KU-077-379

SCIENTIFIC ASPECTS OF THE 1975–76 DROUGHT IN ENGLAND AND WALES

A ROYAL SOCIETY DISCUSSION
ORGANIZED BY SIR CHARLES PEREIRA, F.R.S.,
H. L. PENMAN, F.R.S., O. GIBB AND R. A. S. RATCLIFFE
ON BEHALF OF THE BRITISH NATIONAL
COMMITTEE ON HYDROLOGICAL SCIENCES

HELD ON 28 OCTOBER 1977

LONDON
THE ROYAL SOCIETY
1978

Printed in Great Britain for the Royal Society
at the
University Press, Cambridge

ISBN 0 85403 103 0

First published in *Proceedings of the Royal Society of London*,
series A, volume 363 (no. 1712), pages 1–133

Published by the Royal Society
6 Carlton House Terrace, London SW1Y 5AG

HOUSE OF COMMONS
LIBRARY
CATALOGUED

SCIENTIFIC ASPECTS OF THE 1975–76 DROUGHT IN ENGLAND AND WALES

PREFACE

The importance of maintaining good routine measurements of our environment and especially of our water resources is a matter which the Society had occasion to urge on the Government some 20 years ago. Fortunately, the last 20 years have seen a rapid expansion of the hydrological sciences and of the rational development of water resources in Britain – in every desirable aspect there has been innovation or expansion – so much so that there was plenty to talk about in a discussion meeting on the scientific aspects of the drought of 1975–76. The hard work of the preceding two or three decades had produced enough material to permit discussion: there were measurements from observers and research officers in the field, there were ideas – biological, physical and statistical – to steer attempts at coherent description, interpretation and prediction.

It was awareness of this strong basic requirement for a meeting that encouraged the Society to arrange the one-day discussion meeting. Several learned societies and professional institutions had already held, or arranged, specialist meetings, but it seemed worth while holding yet another to achieve a more synoptic survey. Outstanding natural events soon get overlain by folklore, and the first requirement of those of us charged with arranging the meeting was to ensure that what happened during 1975 and 1976 should be put into numbers, both for hydrological phenomena and for closely dependent technologies. It was hoped that some contributors would be able to include similar evidence for post-drought effects, as recovery or otherwise. Other requirements were fairly self-evident. How does the drought fit into the historical record of dry periods in British weather? What happened elsewhere over the same period? Can any of the 'why?' questions be answered? What lessons are there for the future? It was not intended to discuss climatic change, but some of the evidence presented will probably be used in future arguments about it. Within the time restraint on the meeting, and the limited space of the report, only a sample of the measurements could be given: there are many more on record, and the departments and institutes holding them will readily share them with other research workers.

Some of the progress in recent decades is revealed in the papers and replies to questions, particularly in comparisons with other twentieth century droughts such as those of 1921, 1933–4 and 1943–4. Present-day meteorology in Britain can now call on physical measurements in the upper air, and on a mathematical model of the atmosphere that permits numerical experiments on the effect of a large drought area on the weather over the area. Use of the model and the detailed water balances involves some knowledge of the behaviour of soils and plants in a drought: it was good to find ideas developed in agricultural hydrology round about 30 years ago carried over into the much larger scale of whole catchment behaviour. The same 30 years have seen the emergence of hydrology as an outlet for the professional engineer, and as a challenging research area in several universities.

As part of the forward look, the need for foresight in design got the obvious emphasis, plus comments suggesting that the discussion might help planners to reach better decisions about what to design for – or against. After foresight is turned into engineering works or a system of management, some element of fore-knowledge is desirable to get the best out of them: the job goes on, for it is worth noting that the Society, through the British National Committee, has invited international sponsors to help them in arranging a symposium on hydrological forecasting applied to the operation of systems for water resources (April 1980, Oxford).

July 1978

O. GIBB
H. L. PENMAN
H. C. PEREIRA
R. A. S. RATCLIFFE

CONTENTS

	PAGE
PREFACE	V

R. A. S. RATCLIFFE
Meteorological aspects of the 1975–76 drought   3
Discussion: M. K. MILES, B. RYDZ, E. M. SHAW

R. T. CLARKE AND M. D. NEWSON
Some detailed water balance studies of research catchments   21
Discussion: B. RYDZ, T. M. PRUS-CHACINSKI, A. S. THOM,
P. M. BALCHIN, R. C. GOODHEW, E. B. WORTHINGTON, W. L. JACK

E. S. CARTER
The effects of the drought on British agriculture   43
Discussion: E. B. WORTHINGTON, B. RYDZ

J. B. W. DAY AND J. C. RODDA
The effects of the 1975–76 drought on groundwater and aquifers   55
Discussion: D. J. BURDON

M. J. HAMLIN AND C. E. WRIGHT
The effects of drought on the river systems   69
Discussion: W. L. JACK, B. RYDZ, H. B. JACKSON, R. G. SHARP

A. W. DAVIES
Pollution problems arising from the 1975–76 drought   97

O. GIBB AND H. J. RICHARDS
Planning for development of groundwater and surface water resources   109

SIR CHARLES PEREIRA, F.R.S.
Concluding remarks   131

Proc. R. Soc. Lond. A. **363**, 3–20 (1978)

Printed in Great Britain

Meteorological aspects of the 1975–76 drought

By R. A. S. Ratcliffe†

Formerly Meteorological Office, Bracknell, Berkshire, U.K.

The broad scale meteorological features are examined and it is shown that the drought is related to a variety of factors, including unusual coldness in the North Pacific ocean and over Canada in the winter half-year, upper winds stronger than usual in the Central Pacific, and the quasi-biennial oscillation. Feedback mechanisms involving Atlantic sea temperatures and the drought itself helped to maintain the atmospheric mode. The additional evaporation from a reservoir in Southern England due to extra sunshine, high summer temperature, etc., is estimated. An attempt is made to put the drought into historical perspective, with the conclusion that it appears to be a rare event rather than a symptom of climatic change. Lastly, by using a Meteorological Office general circulation numerical model, it is shown that a large area of dry ground may inhibit rainfall: the dryness of the ground over Western Europe in the 1976 summer may have had this effect.

1. Introduction

The 1975/6 drought in Western Europe has raised a good deal of interest both among scientists trying to ascertain the cause (if this can be done), and among economists, agricultural scientists and hydrologists, who are concerned with the effects of the drought and who are responsible for making plans for the future. All interested parties want to know whether the drought was an isolated event or whether it presages further droughts over the next few decades. As well as describing the meteorology, therefore, this paper includes a few facts about evaporation during the period, draws attention to some associations and possible feedback mechanisms involving the atmosphere, oceans and ice cover which may have contributed to its onset and maintenance and also makes an attempt to put the drought in a historical perspective.

2. Definition

Unless otherwise stated, rainfall events in this paper refer to England and Wales as a whole. The drought is here defined as occurring over the 16 month period May 1975 to August 1976 inclusive. This period is chosen because, although the winter of 1974/5 was rather dry in England and Wales, both March and April 1975 were wet. From then until September 1976 all months except September 1975 were either dry or had average rainfall.

† Present address: Royal Meteorological Society, James Glaisher House, Grenville Place, Bracknell RG12 1BX, U.K.

[3]

The five winters 1971–75 were also rather dry, only that of 1973/74 having rainfall above average. As is well known, it is rainfall in the winter half-year that provides the inflow for our ground water aquifers; during the summer half-year evaporation almost always exceeds rainfall. In the spring of 1975, therefore, although most reservoirs were at full capacity, reserves of ground water were already rather low.

3. METEOROLOGICAL DESCRIPTION

Figure 1, which indicates the percentage of rainfall that occurred over the drought period, gives an idea of the extent of the phenomenon and its severity in different places. Over England and Wales as a whole the 16 month period had about 10 % less rain than was recorded over any other 16 month period since 1820 and it was without doubt the driest such period since records began in 1727. The severest drought was in central southern England and northern France but much of Europe was affected to some extent.

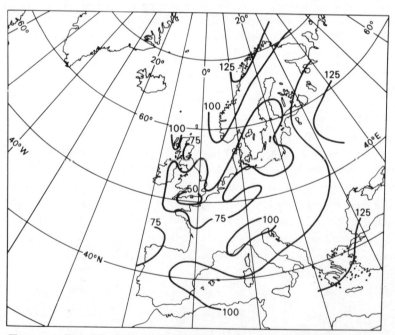

FIGURE 1. Rainfall over the period May 1975 to August 1976 inclusive expressed as a percentage of the 16 month average.

In considering the meteorology of the drought it will not be possible to give the day-to-day meteorological detail that can be obtained from the Meteorological Office Daily Weather Reports but there were many unusual factors that showed considerable persistence. Some of these have been described by Miles (1977) and Ratcliffe (1977a).

Firstly, in addition to their dryness, the winters 1971–4 were all mild, not only in Britain but over most of Europe as far east as Moscow and also in the Russian Arctic. As a result, the coldest air in the Northern Hemisphere was displaced westwards to Canada and the North Pacific, where winters were all notably colder than the 1951–70 averages (Painting 1976).

The second interesting fact is that the jet stream in the east Atlantic/European sector was displaced between 5 and 10 degrees of latitude northwards over the

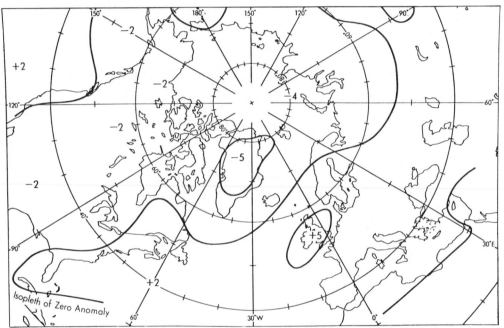

FIGURE 2. Isopleths of surface pressure anomaly (mbar†) from the 1951–70 average during the period May 1975 to August 1976 inclusive.

16 month drought period compared with the same 1951–70 averaging period. This northward movement occurred in the late autumn of 1974 and, on a monthly basis, was persistent, with only short period variations until September 1976, suggesting a good deal of inertia in the atmosphere over this 16 month period (Morris & Ratcliffe 1976). Displacement of the jet stream to a position north of the British Isles invariably leads to more anticyclonic weather over Britain on the day-to-day time scale and effectively results in the depressions that bring rain being diverted northwards into Scandinavia and northwest Russia as happened in the period we are discussing. Figure 2, showing the mean sea-level pressure anomaly over the 16 month period, illustrates these facts.

Thirdly, it is noticeable that the Pacific Ocean north of 40° N was continuously colder than usual, especially from spring 1975 to summer 1976 inclusive. Figure 3

† 1 mbar = 100 Pa.

shows the mean anomaly of sea temperature per $5 \times 5°$ latitude/longitude quadrangle over the whole North Pacific north of $40°$ N since the summer of 1974. It is probable that the coldness of the ocean was partly due to the coldness of the winters of the early 1970s in that sector of the hemisphere: in particular, ice was excessive in the North Pacific in late winter 1975 and 1976, and its melting may well have been partly responsible for the sharp increase of negative sea temperature anomalies in the springs and summers of those years. Note the return of sea temperatures to near normal in 1977.

The upper wind speed at 500 mbar was computed for the drought period over the hemisphere north of $15°$ N and compared with the average at each latitude/longitude intersection point on the standard grid. There were three areas where the flow was significantly different (at the 5 % level with the use of the t test) from average. Two of these were, as one would expect, in regions to the north and south of the British Isles where the flow was significantly stronger and weaker respectively, reflecting the northward displacement of the jet stream. The third area was at $45°$ N in the east Central Pacific between 150 and $180°$ W: here the mean flow

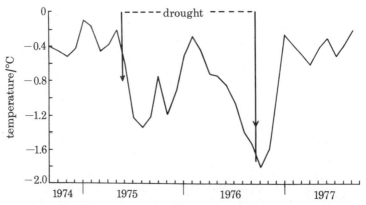

FIGURE 3. North Pacific sea temperature anomalies: mean anomaly north of $40°$ N from $150°$ E to American coast, relative to long-period average.

was 4 m/s stronger than the average of 17 m/s, an enhancement of more than 20 % over the 16 months as a whole. The time series of the anomalous flow at the midpoint of the area is shown in figure 4. Since there was also considerable enhancement of the atmospheric temperature gradient from north to south in the Pacific during the drought, it seems highly probable that the cold water north of $40°$ N was a factor contributing to the increased atmospheric temperature gradient and hence to the enhanced flow, especially as sea temperatures south of $40°$ N were not in general colder than usual.

The relation between strong air flow in the Central Pacific near $45°$ N and weather over Britain was examined more closely by selecting the 14 summers since 1873 when surface flow between $35°$ and $55°$ N and 150 and $180°$ W was noticeably enhanced, and comparing with the eight summers when flow was noticeably decreased in the same area. The mean summer rainfall over England and Wales for the 'enhanced' sample was 196 mm while that for the 'decreased' sample was 265 mm, a difference significant at the 5 % level. The 'enhanced' sample mean was significantly more anticyclonic than the 'decreased' sample mean, while 12 of the 14 'enhanced' sample years had good summers over Britain compared with only one good summer in the 'decreased' sample, as measured by the index of cyclonicity (Murray & Lewis 1966).

The enhanced Pacific flow and the winter coldness over Canada appear to have been important factors in the drought. The hemispheric 500 mbar flow pattern can be resolved into its major orthogonal component patterns by eigenvector methods. One can then select the component patterns that represent enhanced Pacific flow and enhanced flow around the east Canadian trough and compound them to see what are the normal downstream consequences. For the two month season January–February the resulting 500 mbar anomaly pattern is shown in figure 5,

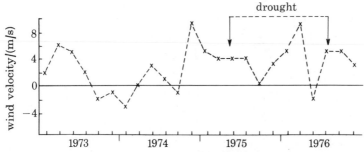

FIGURE 4. Anomalies of the 500 mbar zonal component of geostrophic wind at 45° N, 170° W relative to 1951–70 average (17 m/s) (two-month season values).

which may be compared with the actual anomaly pattern for January/February 1976 (figure 6). There is clearly a good deal of similarity, indicating a connection between the enhanced Pacific and Canadian flow and the anomalous ridge over western Europe. In fact the technique is able to show that what happened over Europe in the winter half year 1975/6 was the normal concomitant of flow stronger than usual in the Pacific and over eastern Canada. In summer, when wavelengths were shorter, a 500 mbar ridge developed over east Canada in both 1975 and 1976 so that the east Canadian flow was decreased. Figure 7 shows the 500 mbar anomaly pattern that results from adding together those flow patterns that represent this state of affairs, which compares closely with the actual anomaly pattern for summer 1976 (figure 8). The anomaly pattern for summer 1975 was also very similar.

In addition to the factors already mentioned, there were almost certainly feedback reactions on the atmosphere through the Atlantic sea temperature anomaly patterns during the drought. In the summers of both 1975 and 1976,

R. A. S. Ratcliffe (Discussion Meeting)

ocean temperatures to the east and southeast of Newfoundland were in general lower than usual. Ratcliffe & Murray (1970) showed that such patterns of sea temperature are normally followed by rather blocked anticyclonic situations over Britain. The cold ocean itself may well have owed its origin to the unusual winter and spring coldness over east Canada which, with the prevailing westerly circulation, would be likely to cool the adjacent ocean more than in the normal year. In the winter half-year 1975/6 the Atlantic was colder than usual north of about

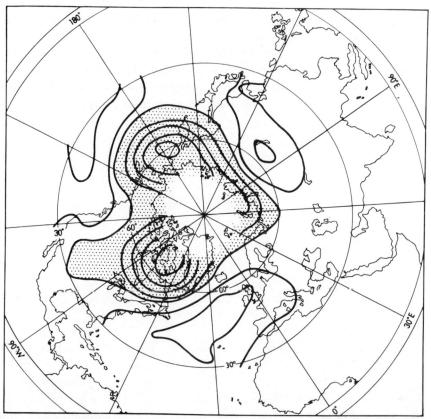

Figure 5. Compound of 500 mbar eigenvector patterns showing enhanced Pacific and enhanced Canadian trough: two month season, January–February. Arbitrary units (negative values shaded).

55° N, due perhaps to the excessive cyclonic activity south of Iceland. Such a sea temperature anomaly pattern has been shown to favour an anomalous ridge extending towards Britain from the Azores anticyclone much as actually happened in the winter of 1975/76.

Yet another interesting fact is that most of the drought period was associated with the westerly phase of the quasi-biennial oscillation (q.b.o.) of tropical stratospheric winds. This phase started in spring 1975 and continued until early summer

1976. Ebdon (1975) has shown that the Atlantic jet stream is usually further north in westerly compared to easterly q.b.o. phases.

About late spring 1976 the broad-scale meteorological situation, which had showed considerable inertia and persistence for over a year, was showing signs of a change. Extra baroclinicity became apparent in the upper flow in mid Atlantic near 50° N, possibly as a consequence of cold water in the Davis Strait region coming southeast into the Atlantic, and the main jet stream had reached an

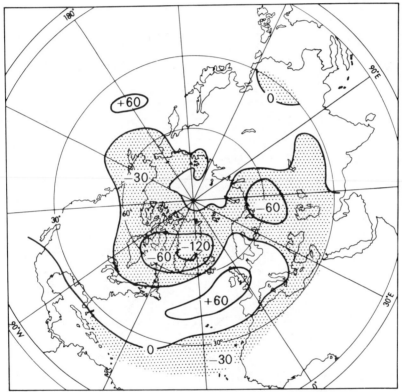

FIGURE 6. Anomalies of 500 mbar geopotential surface (geopotential metres) relative to 1951–70 average: two month season, January–February 1976 (negative values shaded).

extremely far north position near Iceland. The westerly phase of the q.b.o. was also about to end and indeed all seemed set for a breakdown of the long standing régime and a transfer of the jet stream to near 50° N. The upper flow in the Pacific at 45° N had also weakened (see figure 4). All the statistical evidence, on which the experimental summer forecast for 1976 prepared in the Synoptic Climatology Branch of the Meteorological Office was based, suggested a breakdown to a normal unsettled summer pattern.

It is my view that the weather did not break at this stage primarily because of the drought itself (perhaps aided by the resurgence of Pacific flow: see figure 4). It has been demonstrated (Ratcliffe 1976) that the excessive dryness of the ground in the late spring and early summer resulted in about 90 % of the daily net radiation being available for heating the ground and thence the air: in a normal year sensible heat transfer accounts for about 60% of the daily net radiation with approximately 40% used in evaporation. The favourable anticyclonic situation that developed around 20 June thus resulted in very high temperatures over Britain and western

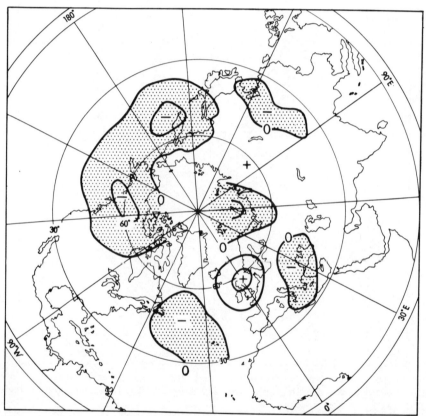

FIGURE 7. Compound of 500 mbar eigenvector patterns showing enhanced Pacific and weak Canadian trough: two month season, July–August. Arbitrary units (negative values shaded).

Europe. The mean temperature anomaly of the 1000/500 mbar layer of the atmosphere over Britain for mid-June to mid-July was in fact about twice that in any other comparable period since the war. This factor seems to have been sufficient to keep Britain on the warm side of the main baroclinic zone and to have allowed the frontal systems of depressions to slide away northwards just to the west of Ireland, effectively maintaining the fine weather and drought until the end of August. When depressions and frontal systems did manage to penetrate near to the British Isles, very little rain developed. The numerical experiments referred to in §6 suggest that this may have been at least partly a consequence of the lack of available moisture over Europe.

With the imminent onset of Arctic cooling, the extreme northern position of the jet stream near Iceland could not be maintained much longer. The increase of thermal gradient noted in the early summer in mid Atlantic around 50° N had, if anything, increased and the most likely event appeared to be a discontinuous evolution so that the main flow would be transferred from the latitude of Iceland

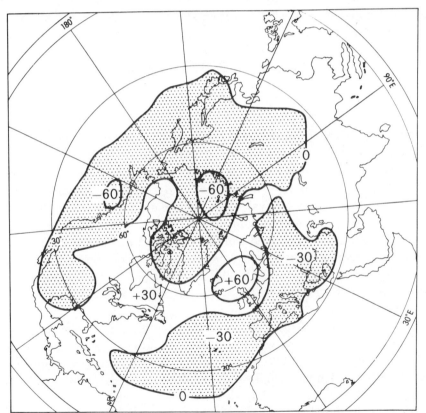

FIGURE 8. Anomalies of 500 mbar geopotential surface (geopotential metres) relative to 1951–70 averages: two month season, July–August 1976 (negative values shaded).

to about 50° N across the Atlantic. This change was initiated by an outbreak of cold air from the Arctic into northern Canada in late August, which started a major retrogression of the Arctic flow pattern and precipitated a cold plunge down the North Sea, which eventually formed a cold trough west of Biscay and resulted in the main upper flow becoming established across the Atlantic near 50° N (Ratcliffe

1977 *b*). This development was unusual and against the normal climatology, because there is often strong persistence of weather in Britain from August to September and, as the general circulation begins its seasonal strengthening, an increase of wavelength is normal. The change of régime resulted in a shortening of wavelength and hence was unusual for the season. Once this major change in the circulation had taken place, the excessive rains of September and October followed. One reason for their exceptional nature was undoubtedly the high sea temperatures (up to 2° C above average) that existed to the southwest of the British Isles due to the long hot summer. Such high ocean temperatures enabled more moisture and more sensible heat to be transferred to the atmosphere than is usual and, given the favourable synoptic situation provided by the upper trough, greatly enhanced the rain producing process. The abnormal difference of sea temperature (about 4° C) existing between about 40° N, 30° W and 35° N, 20° W is also believed to be a factor aiding cyclonic development to the southwest of Britain. To some extent at least therefore it would appear that the exceptional autumn rains of 1976 had their origin in the exceptional summer.

4. Evaporation during the drought

The potential evaporation (Penman 1948) at Kew taking account of the sunshine, wind speed, dryness of the air, etc., over the period May 1975 to August 1976 was 120 % of the long period average (1092 mm compared with the average of 903 mm). Allowing for the lower albedo of a water surface compared to grass at Kew, this is approximately equivalent to 230 mm extra evaporation from a large area of open water such as a reservoir.

During the exceptional hot spell from 23 June to 8 July 1976 when 32 °C was recorded somewhere in England every day for 16 days, the actual evaporation at Kew (tank measurement) was 96.8 mm, almost equal to the amount usually recorded over an average June or July and thus approximately 50 mm more than usual over the 16 days.

Over the summer of 1976 (May–August) potential evaporation at Kew was close to the expected extreme value ever likely to occur as deduced from records over the last 100 years or so (Wales-Smith 1977 *a*). The actual value was 455 mm compared with the long period average of 358 mm. This figure implies about 120 mm more evaporation from large open water areas than in a normal summer and made a small contribution towards the excessive loss from reservoirs.

5. Historical perspective

The mean decadal rainfall at Manchester (since 1791), Kew (since 1700) and Pode Hole, Lincolnshire (since 1731), together with the wettest and driest non-overlapping 16 month periods in each decade (expressed as a percentage of the 16 month average) at each location, are shown in figures 9–11. At Manchester and

Kew the recent period is not the driest in the record: in general, extremes seem to follow the mean curve. There is nothing to suggest a trend towards more extreme droughts except perhaps at Pode Hole. There rainfall appears to show a downward trend since the early 1800s and one might argue that recent rainfall shows a return to the régime of the early 1700s when droughts were more common. However, further investigation suggests that this downtrend is probably not real. Composite records from nearby locations have been examined, e.g. Hull (since 1847), Redmire's reservoir, Sheffield (since 1841), Mansfield (since 1807), Althorpe, Northants (since 1841), Cambridge (since 1848) and Norwich (since 1836). All these places show similar variations of rainfall over the record but none share the

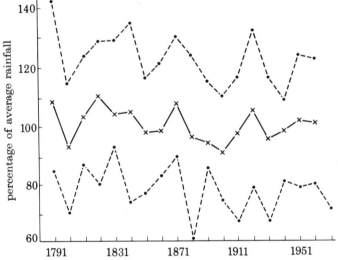

FIGURE 9. Mean decadal rainfall and wettest and driest 16 month periods in each decade at Manchester expressed as a percentage of the long period average.

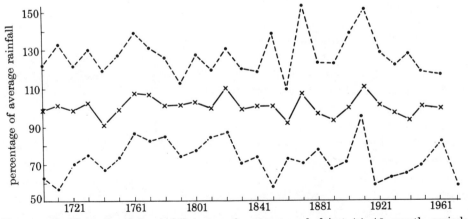

FIGURE 10. Mean decadal rainfall (×) and wettest and driest (•) 16 month periods in each decade at Kew expressed as a percentage of the long period average.

downward trend observed at Pode Hole. Mansfield is typical and its decadal means are included in figure 11 for comparison with Pode Hole. The records are remarkably similar: only the trend is different. Deductions of an increasing probability of droughts in the future based on the apparent decline in rainfall at Pode Hole are therefore probably erroneous.

As another method of looking at the problem of drought frequency, the potential soil moisture deficit (defined as potential evaporation minus rainfall) has been examined for Kew for the period April–August since 1697. Annual totals and 10 year running means show no trend although 1976 is the highest individual value (Wales-Smith 1977*b*). Again, therefore, there is no suggestion of a recent trend towards more frequent droughts.

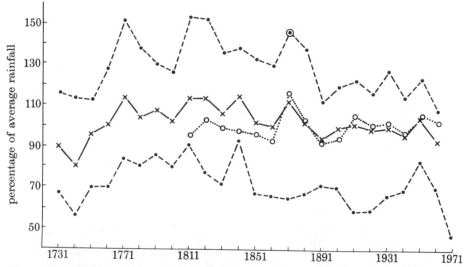

FIGURE 11. Mean decadal rainfall at Pode Hole (×) and Mansfield (○) and wettest and driest 16 month periods in each decade at Pode Hole (•) expressed as a percentage of the long period average.

More recently an investigation into the variation in the frequency of exceptional rainfall anomalies over the last century, using various averaging periods from 5 days to a year, has been carried out on records from several English stations (Ratcliffe, Weller & Collison 1978). This research shows that the frequency of exceptional rainfall anomalies is not a maximum in recent years for any averaging period considered. The only noteworthy factor observed was that, over periods of three months, 1975 and 1976 were very exceptional. A similar investigation of exceptional anomalies of surface pressure shows that these, too, have not become more common over any averaging period recently. It would appear therefore that the drought, and 1976 in particular, were very unusual but there is no evidence of a climatic change or trend towards more frequent such unusual events in the future.

6. Numerical experiments relevant to the drought

Charney (1975) suggested that changes of albedo could be an important factor in maintaining or creating deserts. He postulated that lack of rainfall leading to lack of vegetation will result in a higher albedo. The consequent radiation deficit requires sinking motion to maintain the heat balance and this leads to anticyclonic conditions, additional drying and thus maintenance of the *status quo*.

Berkofsky (1976) applying these ideas to data acquired in the Negev Desert in 1974 showed that sinking motion did occur in his desert circulation model when the albedo was high, and rising motion took place with lower albedoes. The implication is that a lowering of the albedo over deserts could lead to increased vertical velocity at the top of the boundary layer and hence perhaps to more rainfall.

Albedo depends on vegetation and therefore on ground wetness. The albedo of bare soil is linearly related to the water content of the top layers varying from about 0.30 if the soil is completely dry to 0.14 if saturated. Charney's ideas therefore depend on soil moisture, but in addition the amount of moisture in the soil may influence the weather more directly. This may occur because soil moisture effects evaporation and hence changes the proportion of net incoming radiation available as latent heat compared to that available as sensible heat.

Walker & Rowntree (1977) recently reported two numerical experiments using a simple version of the Meteorological Office tropical model. They used a simple zonally symmetrical land–sea distribution with land surface initially wet (W case) and then part wet part dry (D case). Albedo, radiation budget and all other aspects of the model were kept the same in order to isolate the response of the model to soil moisture. The area covered was 36° N to 16° S and 0–32° E, and model variables were specified on a $2 \times 2°$ latitude/longitude grid. Radiative heating was assumed constant at 150 W/m². Evaporation was estimated in two phases. First, actual evaporation, E_A, was assumed to be equal to the potential value, E_T, while the available water in the root layer of vegetation was more than half of its maximum value (taken as 10 cm). Then, for residual available water in the range $5 > \theta > 0$ cm, the ratio E_A/E_T was taken as $\theta/5$.

The model area was divided into two parts to approximate to the real Africa, namely land north of 6° N and sea south of 6° N (see figure 12). In the D case it was assumed there was no soil moisture in the band 14–32° N (approx. the Sahara) and for the remaining land 10 cm soil moisture was assumed. In the W case, 10 cm soil moisture was assumed for all land.

All initial meteorological fields were zonally symmetrical except for a sinusoidal meridional wind component varying with height with maximum amplitude 3 m/s and wave length 32° (i.e. one wave in the field of computation). These conditions approximated to those found in an easterly wave.

The experiments were run for 10 model days (D case) and 20 model days (W case). The partitioning of energy between latent heat of evaporation and sensible heat flux was found to be determined by the dryness of the ground and by surface temperature. Extra warming of the atmosphere due to higher sensible heat flux (D case) was found to be confined to levels below 500 mbar.

In the two experiments results were very different. In the D case depressions formed about 17° N and moved westwards, but they were shallow features confined to below 750 mbar. In the W case, after 4 days in which the moisture balance adjusted to the surface conditions, a significant change took place: a depression broke away from its initial position near 11° N, moved northwards and developed.

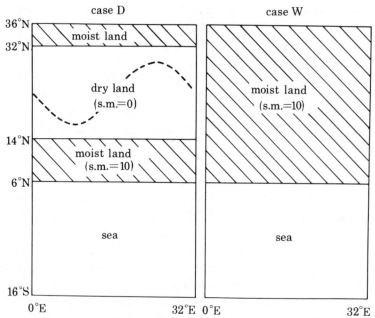

FIGURE 12. Model surface moisture (s.m.) conditions (centimetres).
(a) Case D; (b) case W.

This low had a very different structure from that of the D case, it was much more like an ordinary oceanic depression with inflow near the ground and outflow at 250 mbar and a well marked warm core, due no doubt to latent heat release following convection. Rainfall amounts for the two cases are shown in figure 13. Detailed study of the two cases showed that the energy budgets were quite different. In the D case the depressions derived their energy mainly from the north–south temperature gradient while in the W case latent heat release following convection was the main energy source.

Basically the experiments suggest positive feedback: soil moisture in the W case aids rainfall which maintains the soil moisture; soil dryness in the D case inhibits rainfall allowing persistence of the dry régime. These facts may be relevant to Sahel droughts, indicating that once unusual dryness has become established and perennial vegetation damaged, a recurrence of drought the following year is more likely. Also, if short-rooted vegetation is poorly developed due to dryness early in the season, then perhaps dryness is more likely to persist throughout that season. Analysis of the persistence of droughts in the Sahel shows a tendency for year to year persistence greater than would be expected by chance; Bunting, Dennett, Elston & Milford (1975) have shown that there is some association between Sahel

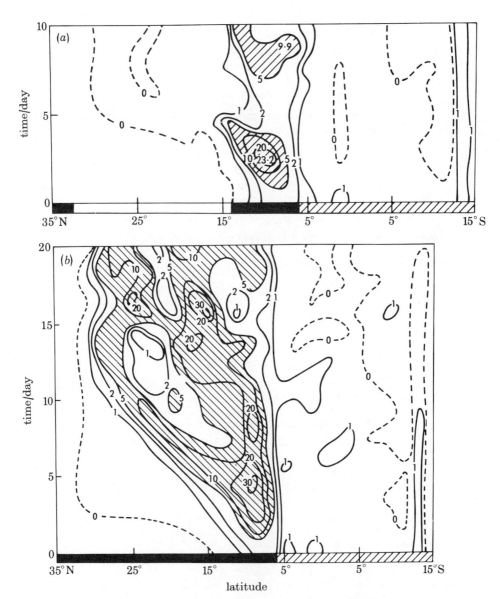

FIGURE 13. Variation with time of zonal mean rainfall (millimetres per day). The nature of the underlying surface is indicated by shading along the latitude axis (dry land, white; moist land, black; ocean, black). (*a*) Case D; (*b*) case W.

dryness in June and dryness later in the same season. Such persistence, however, may not be caused primarily by either the amount of surface moisture or by high albedo: it could be instigated, for instance, by long-term variations of ocean temperature.

Nevertheless, these model experiments are relevant to the European drought of 1975/76 since the area concerned was quite large and may well have reduced the raininess of those disturbances which did manage to penetrate into the area. This was most probable after mid-July when several frontal systems crossed the area without giving any appreciable rainfall.

7. Conclusion

The investigations outlined above suggest that the drought was the result of complicated interaction between a number of large-scale meteorological and oceanographic factors. Feedback mechanisms involving ocean temperatures in the Atlantic and Pacific and also the dryness of the ground itself probably helped to maintain the atmospheric mode longer than it otherwise would have done.

There appears no evidence to suggest a climatic change or trend; rather the drought stands out as an isolated but very unusual event.

Almost all of the work described in this paper was carried out in the Meteorological Office and I am very grateful to my recent colleagues in the Synoptic Climatology Branch, especially M. K. Miles, R. C. Tabony and J. D. Lankester. My thanks are also due to B. G. Wales-Smith who provided most of the data on evaporation.

References (Ratcliffe)

Berkofsky, L. 1976 The effect of variable surface albedo on the atmospheric circulation in desert regions. *J. appl. Met.* **15**, 1139–1144.

Bunting, A. H., Dennett, M. D., Elston, J. & Milford, J. R. 1975 Seasonal rainfall forecasting in West Africa. *Nature, Lond.* **253**, 622–623.

Charney, J. G. 1975 Dynamics of deserts and drought in the Sahel. *Q. Jl R. met. Soc.* **101**, 193–202.

Ebdon, R. A. 1975 The quasi-biennial oscillation and its association with tropospheric circulation patterns. *Met. Mag.* **104**, 282–297.

Miles, M. K. 1977 Atmospheric circulation during the severe drought of 1975/76. *Met. Mag.* **106**, 154–163.

Morris, R. M. & Ratcliffe, R. A. S. 1976 Under the weather. *Nature, Lond.* **264**, 4–5.

Murray, R. & Lewis, R. P. W. 1966 Some aspects of the synoptic climatology of the British Isles as measured by simple indices. *Met. Mag.* **95**, 193–203.

Painting, D. J. 1976 A study of some aspects of the climate of the Northern Hemisphere in recent years. *Met. Off. Sci. Pap.* no. 35.

Penman, H. L. 1948 Natural evaporation from open water, bare soil and grass. *Proc. R. Soc. Lond.* A **193**, 120–145.

Ratcliffe, R. A. S. 1976 The hot spell of late June–early July 1976. *Weather* **31**, 355–357.

Ratcliffe, R. A. S. 1977a A synoptic climatologist's viewpoint of the 1975/76 drought. *Met. Mag.* **106**, 145–153.

Ratcliffe, R. A. S. 1977*b* The wet spell of September–October 1976. *Weather* **32**, 36–37.

Ratcliffe, R. A. S. & Murray, R. 1970 New lag associations between N. Atlantic sea temperature and European pressure applied to long range weather forecasting. *Q. Jl R. met. Soc.*
96, 226–246.

Ratcliffe, R. A. S., Weller, J. & Collison, P. 1978 Variability in the frequency of unusual
weather over approximately the last century. *Q. Jl R. met. Soc.* **104**, 243–255.

Wales-Smith, B. G. 1977*a* An analysis of monthly potential evaporation totals representative of Kew from 1698–1976. *Met. Mag.* **106**, 297–313.

Wales-Smith, B. G. 1977*b* Potential soil moisture deficit at Kew 1698–1976. Evap. Memo
No. 38 (unpublished document available in Nat. Met. Library, Bracknell).

Walker, J. & Rowntree, P. R. 1977 The effect of soil moisture on circulation and rainfall in
a tropical model. *Q. Jl R. met. Soc.* **103**, 29–46.

Discussion

M. K. MILES (*Meteorological Office, Bracknell, Berks, U.K.*). I wish to make two
points concerning the relation between the Pacific circulation and the weather in
the British Isles in summer.

The first is a comment on the statistical basis for the relation beteeen the upper
flow in the Pacific Ocean and the character of the summer circulation in the area
of the British Isles.

Among the highest correlations is one of 0.53 between an index of the 500 mbar
flow between 35° and 55° N and from 170 to 130° W, and an objective index of
anticyclonicity over the British Isles, If, however, the summers of 1975 and 1976,
which prompted the hypothesis, are removed, the correlation falls to 0.36 which
for 14 pairs of observations has rather a low statistical significance.

The second point is to show how sensitive the rainfall over England is to small
changes in the circulation pattern. The 500 mbar index for the E. Pacific for the
summer of 1977 was (like that for 1976) well above average and the anticyclonicity
index for the British Isles was also above average, if only slightly. However, the
rainfall pattern over England was in marked contrast to that of summer 1976 –
southern districts having above average rainfall and northern districts below – the
gradient of rainfall percentage being reversed compared with summer 1976.

R. A. S. RATCLIFFE. I agree with both Mr Miles's points: however, the 500 mbar
flow in the Pacific in the summers of 1976 and 1977 was somewhat different
although the index was similar. It is encouraging that both summers had anticyclonic anomalies near the British Isles although the position of these anomalies
was different and hence the gradient of rainfall over U.K.

B. RYDZ (6 *Kingsdown House, Box, Corsham, Wiltshire, SN*14 9*AX, U.K.*). I am
glad that Mr Ratcliffe has helped to discourage the notion of climatic change. If
the engineer were to believe in the likelihood of trends of change this would of
course add one more uncertainty in an area he deals with only partly rationally and
partly by well-established conventions. It is not easy to see what rational response
he should make to this or how he would take the political decision makers along

with him. Rapid trends of change can hardly be distinguished (except in retrospect) within the pattern of random events whereas accepting a gradual decline in reliability, which is chosen subjectively anyway, seems the most sensible reaction to a suspected slow trend until firmer evidence accumulates.

Miss E. M. SHAW (*Department of Civil Engineering, Imperial College, London, U.K.*). In order to study climatic variability, and in particular the incidence of droughts, the long-period records of rainfall at Kew, Manchester and Edinburgh are invaluable. An objective method of drought definition from monthly rainfall, accounting for seasonal variations and carry-over effects from one month to another, has been applied to the Kew record 1697–1976. Indices of drought severity, incorporating intensity and duration, show that the 1921 drought was the most severe at Kew in 280 years. The 1976 drought ranked eighth in severity. A similar analysis of the Manchester and Edinburgh records 1786–1976 indicated wide variability over the last 191 years and indeed the 1976 drought did not appear at Manchester. Would it be possible to investigate further the meteorological situations pertaining at the time of previous notable droughts, especially in 1921? Perhaps research into sea temperatures in the eighteenth and nineteenth centuries might also be rewarding.

The variability in the severity of some recent droughts over England and Wales was demonstrated from rainfall records of 1911–76. Would a look into the interaction of local characteristics and the mesoscale meteorological situations help to explain regional differences?

R. A. S. RATCLIFFE. I think it would be difficult to carry out a proper investigation of the meteorological situations leading up to and during the 1921 drought: upper-air data and ocean temperature data for the Pacific are not available. Similar remarks apply to droughts which occurred in the eighteenth and nineteenth centuries.

Regional differences of drought severity can be explained in terms of the meteorological situations obtaining at the time.

Proc. R. Soc. Lond. A. **363**, 21–42 (1978)

Printed in Great Britain

Some detailed water balance studies of research catchments

By R. T. Clarke and M. D. Newson

Institute of Hydrology, Wallingford, OX10 8BB, U.K.

Aspects of the water balance during the drought period 1975–76 are reported for the Institute of Hydrology's experimental catchments in Cumbria, East Anglia, the Thames Valley and upland Wales. Summer (April–September) and winter (October–March) totals of precipitation, streamflow and potential evaporation during the drought were compared with mean values for seasons preceding it; where soil moisture was measured by neutron probe, losses from actual evaporation were also compared. Yield dropped proportionately less in relation to rainfall where catchments contained appreciable storage, such as the Cam catchment in East Anglia with its chalk–glacial drift aquifer, or the Wye and Severn catchments in upland Wales which contain storage areas of peat underlain with glacial drift. The stream draining the Oxford clay of the Ray catchment in the Thames valley, on the other hand, dried up entirely in the second summer of the drought.

The paper suggests that the comparison of water yields from the Wye and Severn catchments, which are under hill pasture and coniferous forest respectively, gives results which have considerable bearing on the future management of water resources from upland areas when the aim of management is to maintain supplies of water even during periods of drought as extreme as the years 1975–76. The effect on reservoir operation of neglecting to allow for change in land use is illustrated by a hypothetical example using an artificial 30 year streamflow sequence containing a drought year with very long return period.

1. The assessment of drought severity

A study of drought severity may take either of two forms. First, an index of severity, such as the depth of precipitation falling over a period, may be calculated and its frequency of occurrence assessed by comparison with observed precipitation in other years; if plausible assumptions about the probability distribution of precipitation totals are possible, the drought may be described as that occurring with a frequency of once in T years, in the long run. Secondly, the spatial variability in the drought index (such as precipitation depth) may be studied, and the drought severity in one region compared with that in others; such an approach makes no statement of the frequency of drought occurrence.

In this paper, drought severity is assessed in a form intermediate between those described above. The effects of the 1975–76 drought are described in four areas of England and Wales, two upland and two lowland, these areas containing experimental catchments within which the Institute of Hydrology measures components of water balance. The maximum length of streamflow record is twelve years; the

[21]

calculation of return periods (as required for the first of the two approaches described above) would therefore be difficult to justify, while the limited geographical distribution of the experimental sites precludes a full description of spatial variability of the drought. Nevertheless, measurements of streamflow, meteorological variables and, in some places, soil moisture status as well as precipitation, permit some assessment of drought severity within the experimental catchments.

This paper also considers how a change in land use may affect the ability of a water resource system to meet the demands made on it. Water resource planners may design and operate their abstractions from surface water streams and groundwater so that demands can be satisfied even during an extreme drought; if, after definition of the appropriate operating rules, significant changes in land use occur, it is possible that these changes may modify the hydrological behaviour of catchment areas, and if the effect of the land-use change is substantially to reduce volumes of runoff (as where coniferous forest replaces sheep pasture in upland areas where rain falls frequently) the ability of the system to meet demand during the design drought may be threatened. The paper illustrates this by reference to results from the Institute's intensive study in upland Wales of the hydrological consequences of coniferous afforestation.

2. THE CATCHMENTS

In the years since 1964 the Institute of Hydrology has instrumented a number of experimental catchments (shown in figure 1) for the purpose of assessing the effects of alternative land use on water yield.

The Ray and Cam catchments are broadly representative of the South and East of the country, where relatively favourable climate and soil conditions allow considerable choice of agricultural enterprise. The two catchments differ in that the chalk and drift underlying the Cam catchment imply the existence of a significant groundwater term in the water balance equation relating incoming precipitation to streamflow, evaporation and change of water storage in soil and aquifer; with the Jurassic clay of the Ray catchment, on the other hand, this term is almost certainly negligible, most change in storage being restricted to the upper few centimetres of soil. The Coal Burn and Plynlimon catchments are broadly representative of the wetter West and North of England and Wales where the choice of agricultural enterprise is largely restricted either to hill pasture of relatively low productivity, or to timber production from coniferous forest plantations. Both Coal Burn and the Plynlimon catchments were set up to study the effects of these alternatives on water yield and its distribution in time.

Table 1 shows the physical characteristics of the catchments, together with the length of record available from each. In every catchment, river level is continuously recorded for subsequent conversion to discharge by means of theoretical and empirical relations between stage (level) and discharge; precipitation is measured

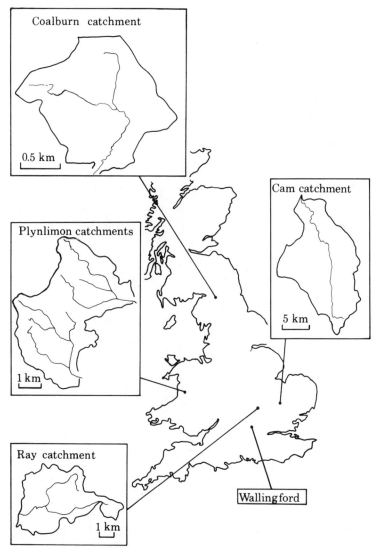

FIGURE 1. Institute of Hydrology research catchments from which records for the drought period are used in this paper.

at a network of gauges read daily, weekly or monthly, and most catchments have at least one autographic raingauge. Meteorological observations are recorded either at a standard (daily) site or at intervals of 5 min by automatic weather stations. On the Plynlimon catchments, soil moisture is recorded by the neutron scattering method.

Meteorological observations at Wallingford have been collected since 1962, and these records are the longest at any of the Institute's sites. In the tables shown in §3 below, the mean values of precipitation and E_T at Wallingford have been included for comparison, although there is no streamflow record for that site.

TABLE 1. INSTITUTE OF HYDROLOGY EXPERIMENTAL CATCHMENTS: PHYSICAL CHARACTERISTICS AND DATA AVAILABILITY

catchment and grid reference	area/km²	channel slope m/km	1916–50 average annual rainfall mm	rock, soils	vegetation, land use	precipitation, streamflow and potential evaporation, E_T from the year	soil moisture measured
Cam at Dernford (TL 466506)	198.0	2.2	603	calcareous brown earths over chalk; brown earths over boulder clay	mixed farming	1966	no
Coal Burn (NT 693777)	1.52	25.2	1143	humic gleys and peat over boulder clay	recently planted coniferous forest	1967	no
Ray (SP 680211)	18.6	4.8	660	mainly gleyed clays overlying Oxford clay (Jurassic)	mixed farming	1964	yes†
Severn (SN 850872)	8.70	63.5	2449	peaty gley podzols and creep brown earths developed on Palaeozoic mudstones and derived tills	mature coniferous forest	1970‡	yes
Wye (SN 829838)	10.5	37.2	2532		hill pasture, partly improved	1969	yes

† Available for years 1964–1973 only.   ‡ Reliable streamflow since 1972.

3. The effect of the drought on individual components of the water balance

This section discusses the components of water balance on the Institute's experimental catchments for the periods April–September 1975, October 1975– March 1976, April–September 1976 and October 1976–March 1977. For brevity, such periods will be called summer 1975, winter 1975–76, and so on. For each water balance component (precipitation, streamflow, soil moisture, actual evaporation) and also for Penman's estimate of potential evaporation, E_T, values recorded during the summer and winter periods of the two drought years are compared with the corresponding mean value derived from earlier years of record; averages therefore exclude data from the extreme years.

TABLE 2. COMPARISON OF PRECIPITATION (millimetres) RECORDED AT FIVE EXPERIMENTAL CATCHMENTS WITH MEAN OF PRECEDING YEARS

Figures in parentheses denote numbers of years of record, in the first column, or percentages of seasonal means, in the second and third columns.

site or catchment	mean, preceding years (April–September)	precipitation, summer 1975	precipitation, summer 1976
Ray	332 ± 55 (11)	259 (78)	188 (57)
Cam	318 ± 78 (9)	288 (91)	177 (56)
Coal Burn	558 ± 74 (8)	642 (116)	449 (81)
Wye	980 ± 163 (6)	858 (88)	554 (57)
Severn	1071 ± 88 (3)	853 (80)	588 (55)
Wallingford	308 ± 51 (13)	240 (78)	200 (65)

site or catchment	Mean, preceding years (October–March)	precipitation, winter 1975–76	precipitation, winter 1976–77
Ray	309 ± 65 (11)	128 (41)	477 (154)
Cam	282 ± 71 (9)	142 (50)	414 (147)
Coal Burn	623 ± 161 (8)	546 (88)	622 (100)
Wye	1466 ± 144 (6)	1227 (84)	1306 (89)
Severn	1474 ± 207 (3)	1216 (82)	1294 (88)
Wallingford	281 ± 55 (13)	122 (43)	438 (156)

(a) Precipitation

Table 2 shows precipitation totals recorded during the four summer and winter seasons spanning the drought years: of the five catchments listed, all but Coal Burn had precipitation below average during the summer of 1975 (values falling in the range 78–91 % of average). In summer 1976, precipitation was well below average in all five catchments (55–81 % of average) and also appreciably less than in summer of the preceding year. The intervening winter was also a period of small precipitation (41–88 % of average), particularly for the catchments in the South and East. During winter 1976–7, when the drought had ended, the Wye and Severn catchments still recorded precipitation below the seasonal average; at all other sites, precipitation equalled the seasonal average (Coal Burn) or greatly exceeded it (Ray).

Table 2 shows nothing of the month to month variation in precipitation. Inspection of monthly totals, and their comparison with corresponding monthly means, shows that (i) the sequence of dry months between April 1975 and August 1976 inclusive, which was apparent for all catchments except Coal Burn, was interrupted only by a September (1975) which was wetter than average; (ii) the record at Coal Burn illustrates a much more variable sequence of wet and dry months, with no sustained dry spell; (iii) for the Plynlimon catchments, the drought had not clearly ended until February 1977: mid-Wales was one of the few parts of the United Kingdom to end 1976 with annual precipitation much below average.

TABLE 3. COMPARISON OF STREAMFLOW (millimetres) RECORDED AT FIVE
EXPERIMENTAL CATCHMENTS WITH MEAN OF PRECEDING YEARS

Figures in parentheses denote numbers of years of record, in the first column, or
percentages of seasonal means, in the second and third columns.

catchment	mean, preceding years (April–September)	streamflow, summer 1975	streamflow, summer 1976
Ray	38 ± 27 (11)	26 (68)	0.4 (0)
Cam	66 ± 20 (9)	96 (145)	26 (39)
Coal Burn	283 ± 50 (7)	370 (131)	198 (70)
Wye	737 ± 153 (6)	557 (76)	315 (43)
Severn	668 ± 17 (3)	416 (62)	225 (34)

catchment	mean, preceding years (October–March)	streamflow, winter 1975–76	streamflow, winter 1976–77
Ray	141 ± 74 (11)	3 (2)	242 (172)
Cam	102 ± 41 (9)	47 (46)	112 (110)
Coal Burn	530 ± 128 (7)	478 (90)	593 (112)
Wye	1286 ± 133 (6)	1172 (91)	1187 (92)
Severn	1182 ± 177 (3)	988 (84)	1013 (86)

(b) Streamflow

Table 3 shows the total streamflow from the five experimental catchments for the two summers and two winters spanning the drought years. As with precipitation, streamflow in summer 1975 was below the seasonal average for the Ray and for the Plynlimon catchments; for the Cam at Dernford Mill, however, streamflow was 45 % above the seasonal average despite the fact that precipitation was 9 % lower than average. The Cam receives a considerable contribution to its flow from groundwater discharging from the underlying chalk, and the large precipitation of winter 1974–75 is likely to have increased water in storage for release during the first of the two drought summers. The extra yield was, however, not sustained through the following winter and summer.

In winter 1975–76, streamflow was below seasonal average in all five catchments, while the Ray all but ceased flowing (streamflow 2 % of seasonal average). In the second summer, 1976, it dried up altogether, while flow in the remaining four catchments varied from 34 % of seasonal average (Severn) to 70 % (Coal Burn).

Streamflow in winter 1976–77 was still below average on the Plynlimon catchments. Figure 2 shows the medians of discharge (expressed per square kilometre of catchment area) from the Wye and Severn catchments for the two drought years and those that preceded them. The figure shows that a median discharge per unit area as small as those recorded on the Wye during the summers of 1975 and 1976 had also occurred in 1971, while a median discharge per unit area smaller than that of winter 1975–76 had occurred in the winter of 1972–73; however, seasonal median discharges were small for a longer period during the drought years than elsewhere in the record.

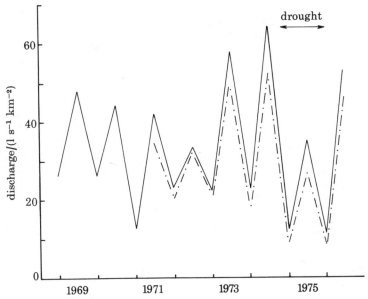

FIGURE 2. Median discharge in 6 month periods (summer, winter) per unit of catchment area: Wye (——) and Severn (— · —) catchments.

Instantaneous minimum streamflow yields in the Plynlimon catchments during August 1976, gauged volumetrically, ranged from over $10 \, \mathrm{l \, s^{-1} \, km^{-2}}$ at the upper ends of both Severn and Wye to around $4 \, \mathrm{l \, s^{-1} \, km^{-2}}$ at the two catchment outfalls. These yields were the highest natural yields reported in Wales (figure 3) although this may reflect the scarcity of upland data. However, yields at Lake Vyrnwy and around Llyn Clywedog, also gauged by Institute staff, seldom exceeded $2 \, \mathrm{l \, s^{-1} \, km^{-2}}$; where they did, there was a clear correlation with extensive deposits of blanket or basin peat.

(c) *Soil moisture*

Although observation well-levels are available for the Cam catchment, abstractions from groundwater complicate their interpretation. For the remaining catchments, soil moisture data were measured in the drought period only for the Wye and Severn catchments, where three lines of tubes inserted into the soil are used for measuring soil moisture by neutron scattering methods. The lines of tubes run perpendicular to the hill slopes: two of them (Cyff and Nant Iago lines) are in the Wye catchments, and the third (Y Foel line) is in the Severn. The tubes penetrate the soil to the underlying bedrock, which is of negligible permeability, and the mean soil depths in the three lines are 90, 60 and 70 cm respectively.

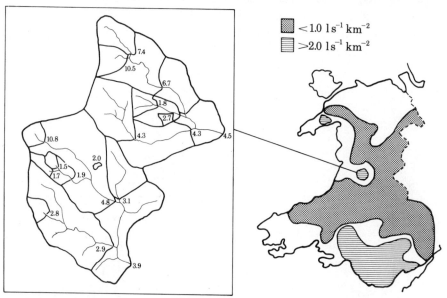

FIGURE 3. Minimum instantaneous discharge yields (summer 1976) for the Wye and Severn catchments (left) and their tributaries in comparison with data available for Wales (right). The map of Wales is based on yields published by the Welsh National Water Development Authority and the Severn–Trent Regional Water Authority.

At each tube, the maximum soil moisture deficit was calculated for summer 1975, winter 1975–76, and summer 1976. This was obtained by (i) calculating the total water content throughout the soil profile for each date (at intervals sometimes of two or three weeks) on which soil moisture was measured; (ii) subtracting the minimum total water content from the water content at 'field capacity', where the latter was determined using soil moisture measurements made two or three days after winter storms, when free-draining water was assumed to have been removed by gravitational forces and a negligible amount had been removed by evaporation. The difference, when averaged over all access tubes in each line, gave the maximum soil moisture deficit, and this was compared with the mean of these maximum deficits recorded in the corresponding season (summer, winter) of preceding years. Table 4 shows that maximum soil moisture deficits in summer 1976 were considerably greater, in percentage terms, than in summer 1975, while maximum soil moisture deficits in both seasons were considerably greater than the mean of the earlier years of record. Furthermore, there is evidence that, for some neutron access tube sites, field capacity levels calculated using data from years before 1975–76 have not since been regained (table 4). This applies particularly to the Y Foel line of tubes in the Severn (forested) catchment.

The Plynlimon catchments can be broadly divided into areas of valley peat, areas of 'blanket' peat on the interfluves, and the steeper hill slopes separating the two where the peat layer, if it exists, is very much shallower; besides computing the maximum soil moisture deficits for each line of access tubes as in table 4, therefore, those access tubes that are all sited in upland blanket peat areas were taken together to derive the maximum soil moisture deficit in such areas within both Wye and Severn catchments. Similarly, tubes occurring in valley peat were considered together, and from the remaining tubes a comparison was obtained between maximum soil moisture deficits in hill slopes under forest and

TABLE 4. MAXIMUM SOIL MOISTURE DEFICITS (millimetres) IN WYE AND SEVERN CATCHMENTS EXPRESSED AS PERCENTAGES (VALUES IN PARENTHESES) OF MEANS OF SEASONAL MAXIMA IN PRECEDING YEARS

	Wye (grass)		Severn (forest)
	Nant Iago	Cyff	Y Foel
	April–September		
1975	110 (157)	86 (218)	53 (238)
1976	160 (228)	132 (330)	118 (530)
1977	77 (110)	37 (91)	62 (280)
	October–March		
1975–76	60 (125)	29 (86)	13 (104)
1976–77	46 (96)	27 (81)	43 (340)

hill pasture. This comparison showed that both forest and pasture slopes were still in deficit in the summer of 1977 after the drought had ended; for pasture slopes, the maximum deficit in that season was 159 % of the mean of summer maximum deficits in pre-drought years, while for forested slopes the figure was 324 %. For both upland peat and valley peat, however, summer maximum deficits in 1977 were similar to those observed in pre-drought years.

Peat areas, together with their underlying drift deposits, play an important storage rôle in the Plynlimon catchments. Analysis of borehole records from peat areas of Plynlimon shows the close relation between water in storage and flow rates when the latter are high; at low flow rates, however, the relation is less well defined. It appears that after 'excess' water has drained off, water yield from the peat itself is very small, and that the large dry-season flows in peat areas (such as those mentioned in §3b above) are sustained from shallow aquifers and drift deposits underlying the peat. This hypothesis is supported by the observation that the relatively high water yields from the Upper Wye and Severn during August 1976 originated in discrete springs in channel banks rather than from diffuse seepage.

Although both upland and valley peat showed maximum deficits in summer 1977 that were little different from those in pre-drought years, some irreversible changes occurred in exposed and shallow peat deposits during summer 1976. Many isolated peat hags became severely cracked and oxidized; when dyed water was put into a borehole, drainage was almost instantaneous, the water emerging through the network of cracks. Cracking and oxidation was also apparent in the thinner peat deposits underlying *Nardus* grassland in the Wye catchment, and this may explain why soils on valley slopes appear to have failed to recover their pre-drought storage capacities.

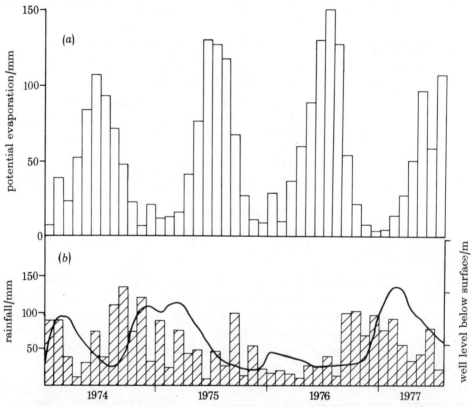

FIGURE 4. Potential evaporation (*a*), rainfall (*b*, histogram) and well levels (*b*, curve) free from bank storage effects, Wallingford meteorological station, 1974–1977.

At Wallingford, observations of groundwater levels in the Thames flood plain have been recorded since 1964. Figure 4 shows a plot of depth of water table below the soil surface for the period June 1974 to July 1977, together with monthly precipitation. The low water table levels for the period November 1975 to October 1976 are readily apparent; in particular, the recharge during the winter months of 1975–76 was not sufficient to raise water table levels to the values recorded either in early 1975 or subsequently in the early months of 1977 after the drought had broken.

(d) *Potential evaporation*, E_T

Table 5 shows values of E_T computed for summer 1975, winter 1975–76, summer 1976 and winter 1976–77 by Penman formula. In both summer seasons, E_T was above seasonal average in all five catchments, and was particularly high at the Wallingford site; E_T was above average in the intervening winter in all catchments except those at Plynlimon. For the winter of 1976–77, E_T was close to the seasonal average. Measured totals of incoming solar radiation were above average for the summer seasons in all five catchments and at the Wallingford meteorological site.

TABLE 5. POTENTIAL EVAPORATION, E_T, IN DROUGHT YEARS FOR FIVE
EXPERIMENTAL CATCHMENTS COMPARED WITH MEANS OF PRECEDING YEARS

Figures in parentheses denote numbers of years of record, in the first column, or percentages of seasonal means, in the second and third columns.

catchment or site	mean, preceding years (April–September)	E_T, summer 1975	E_T, summer 1976
Ray	417 ± 32 (11)	460 (110)	474 (114)
Cam	405 ± 21 (9)	444 (110)	423 (104)
Coal Burn	343 ± 26 (7)	401 (117)	393 (115)
Wye	389 ± 23 (6)	396 (102)	404 (104)
Severn	426 ± 14 (3)	461 (108)	468 (110)
Wallingford	421 ± 25 (9)	511 (121)	518 (123)

catchment or site	mean, preceding years (October–March)	E_T, winter 1975–76	E_T, winter 1976–77
Ray	67 ± 6 (11)	67 (100)	68 (102)
Cam	62 ± 11 (9)	65 (105)	60 (97)
Coal Burn	51 ± 8 (7)	73 (143)	42 (82)
Wye	58 ± 8 (6)	41 (71)	45 (78)
Severn	65 ± 9 (3)	51 (78)	51 (78)
Wallingford	66 ± 12 (9)	72 (109)	67 (101)

(e) *Actual evaporation*, E_A

For a water-tight catchment, the actual loss of water to the atmosphere over a period is given by $P - Q - \Delta S$, where P is precipitation, Q is total streamflow leaving the basin, and ΔS is the change in soil moisture storage over the period. Soil moisture change was recorded by neutron meters only for the Wye and Severn; for these catchments, therefore, actual evaporation for the drought period can be compared with the mean seasonal losses from earlier years of record (table 6).

For both catchments, table 6 shows that actual evaporation in both summer 1975 and summer 1976 was considerably greater than the average for the years of record that preceded the drought period; actual evaporation from the Wye in summer 1976 was at a daily rate slightly greater than in summer 1975, while the converse was true for the Severn. In the intervening winter 1975–76, however, actual evaporation was at a daily rate appreciably less than average in both catchments. Comparison of the seasonal mean actual evaporation losses from the Wye with those from the Severn shows that the latter are the greater.

Losses by actual evaporation from either catchment are the sum of two components: (i) interception losses which, for the Severn in particular, are likely to have been less than the long-term seasonal interception losses because precipitation was below average (table 2 shows that precipitation on the Severn was 80 %, 55 % and 82 % of seasonal average in the seasons summer 1975, winter 1975–76, and summer 1976 respectively) and (ii) losses from soil moisture depletion, which are likely to have been considerably greater than the seasonal mean soil moisture losses (as suggested by table 4, although this presents maximum deficits only).

TABLE 6. ACTUAL EVAPORATION LOSS E_A (millimetres per day) IN DROUGHT YEARS FROM WYE AND SEVERN CATCHMENTS, COMPARED WITH THE SEASONAL MEANS OF PRECEDING YEARS

catchment	mean, preceding years (April–September)	E_A, summer 1975 (18 April–30 Sept.)	E_A, summer 1976 (12 April–19 Sept.)
Wye (pasture)	1.38 ± 0.07	1.70 (123 %)	1.82 (132 %)
(E_T/(mm d^{-1}))	2.14 ± 0.13		
Severn (forest)	1.98 ± 0.21	2.53 (128 %)	2.36 (119 %)
(E_T/(mm d^{-1}))	2.34 ± 0.08		

catchment	mean, preceding years (October–March)	E_A, winter 1975–76 (1 Oct.–11 April)
Wye (pasture)	0.92 ± 0.13	0.44 (48 %)
(E_T/(mm d^{-1}))	0.32 ± 0.04	
Severn (forest)	1.42 ± 0.16	1.21 (85 %)
(E_T/(mm d^{-1}))	0.36 ± 0.05	

Since daily rates of actual evaporation from both catchments were appreciably greater than seasonal average in both drought summers, any reduction in interception losses was more than compensated by the depletion of soil moisture, although this may not have been true for the intervening winter when actual evaporation from the Severn was slightly below the seasonal average.

It is of interest to compare the seasonal mean daily losses by actual evaporation with the mean daily potential evaporation, E_T, estimated by Penman's equation. Both Wye and Severn had daily losses appreciably greater than E_T during the winter 1975–76, despite the fact that the daily loss by actual evaporation from the Wye for that season was only 48 % of the mean of preceding years, and that for the Severn 85 %. In both summers, on the other hand, the Wye had a daily loss smaller than mean seasonal E_T, while the Severn had daily loss greater than mean seasonal E_T. The discrepancy, which is very marked in winter, between mean actual evaporation E_A from the Severn (forested) catchment and mean Penman's E_T illustrates the danger of estimating the seasonal yield from a reservoired catchment under forest, either from precipitation and E_T, or by transferring estimates from a catchment under hill pasture.

4. Inferences for water resource management

Measurements from the experimental catchments shown in §3 give some indication of the regional differences in severity of the drought, and of the resultant effects of low rainfall combined with catchment characteristics on streamflow yield. Yield decreased proportionately less in relation to rainfall on the Cam, with its chalk/drift storage areas, than on the Ray catchment, where storage in the heavy clays is small. The Plynlimon catchments, moreover, have yielded results which, we believe, have considerable bearing on the future management of water resources in upland catchment areas, and the remainder of this paper is concerned with a presentation of the inferences for water resource management that derive from these results.

The agriculturalist and the water resources engineer assess the severity of a drought in different ways; for the former, the reductions in crop yields provide appropriate measures of severity, so that he may take as an index the return period of the rainfall or soil moisture deficit measured during a crop growing season or some critical part thereof. For the water resources engineer responsible for the yield from water catchment areas, and its storage and distribution, drought severity may be quantified in terms of the return period of low streamflow recorded during a season of high demand. Calculation of the latter return period from a streamflow record assumes that the sequence of observed streamflows is statistically stationary, an assumption that will be valid (provided, of course, that precipitation is a stationary process) in areas permanently under a single crop, such as grass, or under crops with similar canopy structure grown in rotation; however, in areas where land use changes from, say, pasture to coniferous forest, which, on maturity, is felled and replanted, the assumption may be open to question because of fluctuating water yields derived from such areas.

The comparison of the water balances of the Wye and Severn catchments has demonstrated the difference between their annual water losses (precipitation minus streamflow); intensive studies on smaller-scale plots have confirmed this difference, have explained it in terms of evaporation of the rainfall intercepted by the forest canopy, and have helped to provide a means of extrapolating results from Plynlimon to other catchments. The principal result from the catchment water balance study is as follows. For the Wye catchment, the mean annual loss for the years 1970–75 inclusive was 18 % of the mean annual precipitation of 2415 mm, while for the Severn, the mean annual loss over the same period was 30 % of its mean annual precipitation, 2388 mm. Moreover, the latter percentage made no allowance for the fact that about one-third of the Severn is unforested; if a statistical adjustment is made to allow for this, mean annual loss from the forested area of the Severn rises to 38 % of mean annual precipitation. The reality of these results has been confirmed by plot studies within the Severn forest on 'natural' lysimeters underlain with impermeable boulder clay. Yet further support comes from an analysis of data from the separately gauged subcatchments within each of the Wye and Severn main catchments; table 7 compares the total annual water losses from the Wye and Severn main catchments with the areally weighted mean loss from the three subcatchments within the Wye (Afon Cyff, Gwy and Nant Iago) and from two subcatchments within the Severn (Nant Tanllwyth, Afon Hore). In the drought years of 1975 and 1976, losses from the Wye catchment under hill pasture were about 20 % of annual precipitation, while those for the Severn were rather more than 30 % of annual precipitation; moreover, the latter figure contains no adjustment for unforested areas within the subcatchments.

TABLE 7. ANNUAL PRECIPITATION P, STREAMFLOW Q AND LOSSES $P-Q$ (millimetres) FOR 1974–76, WYE AND SEVERN CATCHMENTS

Figures in parentheses show $P-Q$ as a percentage of P.

Wye	weighted mean of three subcatchments†			main catchment‡		
	P	Q	$P-Q$	P	Q	$P-Q$
1974	2830	2419	411 (14)	2794	2320	474 (17)
1975	2142	1730	412 (19)	2099	1641	458 (22)
1976	1762	1349	413 (23)	1736	1404	332 (19)
mean	2245	1833	412 (22)	2210	1788	421 (19)

Severn	weighted mean of two subcatchments§			main catchment¶		
	P	Q	$P-Q$	P	Q	$P-Q$
1974	2954	2128	826 (28)	2848	2076	772 (27)
1975	2220	1484	736 (33)	2120	1428	692 (33)
1976	1787	1178	609 (34)	1742	1152	590 (34)
mean	2320	1597	724 (31)	2237	1552	685 (31)

Mean altitudes: †, 525 m; ‡ 505 m; §, 515 m; ¶, 514 m.

To illustrate the magnitude of the additional evaporative loss that results from the evaporation of intercepted water from a forest canopy in a region of heavy and frequent rainfall, take the value of this additional loss to be 250 mm at Plynlimon, although this is probably an underestimate. If the Wye catchment, area 10.55 km² at present under pasture, were entirely under forest, the increase in loss due to evaporation of intercepted water would be sufficient to provide for the entire annual domestic requirement for a town of 43 000 people (say, of the size of Shrewsbury) at 1975 water consumption rates. Expressed another way, the additional annual loss due to the forest would be sufficient to fill just over 5 % of the volume of Clywedog reservoir of 50.006×10^6 m³.

We now attempt to show, by means of an artificial example, how a failure to take account of land-use change from hill pasture to coniferous forest in an upland catchment may nullify a water resource management procedure designed to maintain supplies during an extreme drought. It is assumed that water supplies are drawn from an upland area which, for the period of record, has been under hill pasture; the thin line in figure 5 shows a hypothetical realization of 30 years' annual streamflow with approximately the same mean and year-to-year standard deviation as that observed for the Wye catchment. The 30 year sequence of simulated streamflow in the figure has been constructed so as to include that annual streamflow for the drought year which recurs once in 1000 years in the long

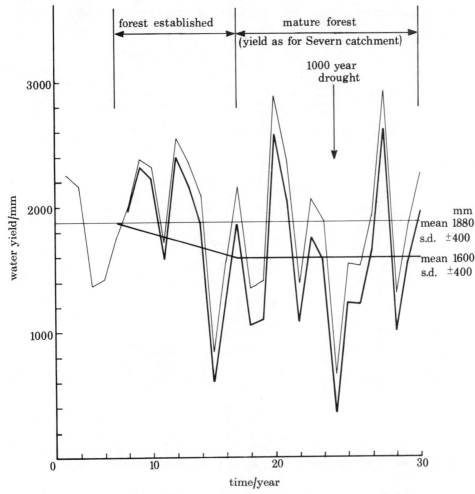

FIGURE 5. Thirty year simulated yields of water from pasture and forest catchments (based on Wye and Severn records).

run; from this sequence, a reservoir may be designed with a volume such that it would just fail to overflow, and just fail to run dry even during the extreme drought, while supplying a demand equal to the mean annual catchment water yield of 1880 mm. Figure 6 (thin line) shows the year-to-year fluctuation in volume of storage within this reservoir.

We now assume that after this reservoir has been constructed, the upland catchment area supplying it is planted to forest in year 5 of the 30 year period; we assume that the forest takes 10 years to develop its full canopy during which annual water yield is reduced linearly, and that thereafter annual water yield is realized according to the thick line of figure 5, giving annual streamflow with the same mean and year-to-year standard deviation as for the Severn catchment. This simulated streamflow sequence also contains an annual streamflow (from the hypothetical forested catchment) for a drought year recurring with a 1000 year

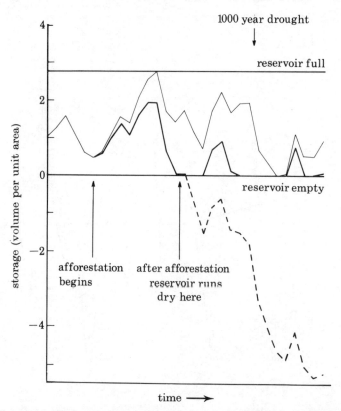

FIGURE 6. Effect of afforestation on a hypothetical reservoir storage where design reservoir draft is taken as the mean annual yield from pasture.

return period. We now consider the behaviour of the reservoir (designed by using data from the catchment when under hill pasture, to supply demand even during the drought year) when the demand remains unchanged, but the water yields are the reduced yields from the forested catchment; the fluctuation of the volume of storage in the reservoir is as shown by the thick line in figure 6. Not only is the reservoir dry when the 1000 year drought occurs, but it has already run dry once before its occurrence. Moreover, it remains dry for much of the remaining period following the drought. Thus it is clear that failure to allow for the land-use change has nullified the resource management procedure designed to maintain supply even during the drought year.

This illustration is, of course, grossly oversimplified or unrepresentative in a number of ways: reservoirs are not designed to give a yield equal to the mean annual streamflow; a year of low rainfall giving water yield with 1000 year return period on a pasture catchment need not necessarily give a yield with the same return period for a catchment under coniferous forest; the example takes no account of within-year storage fluctuation; the artificial sequence of streamflows was generated from a Gaussian distribution, although a case could be made for the use of some other distribution. Nevertheless, it illustrates the fact that afforestation is a factor that must be taken into account when planning to satisfy water demands using supplies from upland catchment areas.

The water industry in Britain has yet to detect the practical effects of afforestation on water yield, and the reason is not far to seek: a survey of land use around major upland reservoirs shows that very few catchment areas yet have any large proportions of forested land. In Wales, for example, Clywedog, Brianne and Brenig have between 30 and 40 % forest cover. However, it is the stated aim of foresters to double the present forest cover in upland areas by the year 2000, and if they are successful, forestry will then occupy just over half our total upland areas. The resultant reduction in water yield may then be more worthy of consideration.

To summarize, therefore, a water resources engineer needs to assess drought severity, not in terms of the return period of small precipitation, but in terms of the return periods of streamflow events; if his resources are from uplands where significant areas are to be forested in the future, resource planning decisions based upon assumptions that do not take account of greater evaporative losses from forest are likely to be in error.

The authors acknowledge with gratitude the contribution to this paper from the Institute's field observers and data processors; without them, this paper could not have been written. Our colleagues, particularly J. R. Blackie and J. P. Bell, provided much constructive advice, and Mrs S. Yaxley deciphered our manuscript with her usual efficiency. We acknowledge with gratitude our Director's permission to publish the paper.

Discussion

B. RYDZ (6, *Kingsdown House, Box, Corsham, Wiltshire, SN14 9AX, U.K.*). I should like to ask Mr Clarke how readily he thinks his conclusions, about the differences in yield–storage–risk relation for afforested and other catchments, can be transposed to droughts of a somewhat different pattern. The differences in evaporation will depend upon a number of factors, such as temperature and sunshine, in addition to rainfall, whereas the extreme drought in his synthetic sequences may have been defined purely in terms of rainfall deficit. Although the other factors are obviously closely associated with this we may have had an exceptional coincidence of low rainfall and high temperature in 1976 and perhaps the separate probabilities should be compounded instead of taking 1976 as a package.

Incidentally, do not the higher than average actual evaporations recorded somewhat contradict Mr Ratcliffe's explanation of the persistence of the drought?

R. T. CLARKE AND M. D. NEWSON. Mr Rydz points out that 'drought' may result either from low rainfall, or from high evaporation, or both, and asks whether the probabilities of these events should not be separated when assessing yield–storage–risk relations by the hypothetical example given in the paper (this example used a synthetic annual streamflow sequence which included a drought year with low flow of long return period). We believe that it is unnecessary for the purpose of our demonstration to separate the probability of low rainfall from that of high evaporation, because the resultant effect of the two factors acting together is the same: namely, low streamflow, which is the variable used in our demonstration because we assumed that it is the component of water balance of principal interest to the water resources engineer.

Mr Rydz also asks whether the actual evaporation recorded at Plynlimon as higher than average does not run counter to Mr Ratcliffe's remarks on the self-perpetuating nature of the drought, such as would be explained by a positive feedback mechanism. We do not see any anomaly here; the actual evaporation figures given in our table 6 are daily means over approximately six month seasons, so that the summer 1976 figure, for example, is calculated using observations from 4 April to 19 September. Any limitation in actual evaporation, occurring when the drought of that summer was at its height, would therefore be masked by actual evaporation rates in the early months of that season and in September. Furthermore, the feedback mechanism described by Mr Ratcliffe (dry soils in late spring, resulting in a greater proportion of incoming solar radiation being available to heat the soil and hence the air, causing high temperatures and high evaporation) was less marked in the Plynlimon catchments, we believe, than in the Southeast and Midlands; rainfall at Plynlimon from October 1975 to March 1976, although below average (table 2), was not as much below average as on the Ray and Cam catchments, while both actual and potential evaporation for that period were below average (tables 5 and 6). Soil moisture at Plynlimon in late spring 1976 may therefore not have been depleted to the same extent as in some other parts of the country.

T. M. PRUS-CHACINSKI (*C. H. Dobbie and Partners, London, U.K.*). The authors have presented us with an extremely neat piece of research and they were careful enough to state that their findings should not be extrapolated to some bigger and geophysically different catchments.

R. T. CLARKE AND M. D. NEWSON. It was a pleasure to hear Dr Prus-Chacinski praise the 'neatness' of our research; however, we did not say (or did not mean to say) that our findings should not be extrapolated to bigger and geologically different catchments. Our point was that where water resource planning decisions concern the estimation of storage required to meet water demands in years of low flows, then estimates may be in error if catchments hitherto under pasture become afforested; the estimates may be wrong because they take no account of the large interception losses from the forest canopy if it is frequently wetted by rainfall. Given estimates of the biological and physical parameters describing forest canopy characteristics, together with good rainfall and meteorological records and some assumptions about canopy behaviour, it is possible to predict both interception and transpiration losses from any catchment subject to afforestation.

A. S. THOM (*Department of Meteorology, The University, James Clerk Maxwell Building, King's Buildings, Mayfield Road, Edinburgh EH9 3JZ, U.K.*). The large evaporative losses from a forested catchment in Wales described by Mr Clarke would probably have been substantially unchanged had the trees been deciduous rather than coniferous. It is the large aerodynamic roughness of forested land rather than the absolute amount of intercepted rainfall held by the trees themselves which leads to the enhanced evaporative losses from forest in contrast to that from grassland (Thom & Oliver 1977).

In relation to the questioned generality of the high evaporative losses reported by Mr Clarke for forested catchment in Plynlimon: these findings can be shown to prescribe an overall framework into which the results from Frank Law's early work in the Yorkshire Pennines (Law 1956) and the Institute of Hydrology's own recent research at Thetford Forest in Norfolk fit in a quite consistent manner. At least up to a mesoscale of several tens of kilometres, it appears that total regional evaporation increases steadily with surface roughness and annual rainfall. Where annual rainfall totals are large, however, adequate runoff must still occur even from totally forested catchments.

References

Law, F. 1956 *J. Br. Waterworks Ass.*, pp. 489–494.
Thom, A. S. & Oliver, H. R. 1977 *Q. Jl R. met. Soc.* **103**, 345–357.

R. T. CLARKE AND M. D. NEWSON. We are grateful to Dr Thom for the clarity with which he pointed out, as we had failed to do, the consistency between the Plynlimon results concerning water use by forests at Plynlimon, Thetford and in the Yorkshire Pennines, as stated by Law.

P. M. BALCHIN (*Leeds*). Would Mr Clarke like to comment on the effect of the intensity, duration and timing of rainfall on interception losses, and the problems posed in trying to extrapolate from mid-Wales to other areas?

R. T. CLARKE AND M. D. NEWSON. Dr Balchin invites us to comment on the effect of intensity, duration and timing of rainfall on interception losses, and the problems posed in trying to extrapolate from mid-Wales to other areas. It is possible to postulate a model of forest canopy behaviour such as that described some years ago by Professor A. J. Rutter (Rutter *et al.* 1971, 1975); this requires knowledge, as stated above, of physical and biological parameters that describe canopy characteristics when it is thoroughly wetted, drying and dry. These parameters will be different for different species (such as those in the deciduous forests mentioned by Professor Russell), but a knowledge of them allows the extrapolation of estimates of interception losses associated with pure stands of that species in any other catchment for which reliable rainfall and meteorological data are available. Estimation of these physical and biological parameters is by no means easy, but techniques for their estimation are under constant development. The interception losses will be strongly dependent on rainfall frequency and intensity; losses will be greater where a forest canopy is wetted frequently, by light rainfall, than where it is wetted infrequently by heavy rainfall, other factors being equal.

References

Rutter, A. J., Kershaw, K. A., Robins, P. C. & Morton, A. J. 1971 *Agric. Met.* **9**, 367–384.
Rutter, A. J., Morton, A. J. & Robins, P. C. 1975 *J. appl. Ecol.* **12**, 367–380.

R. C. GOODHEW (*Severn–Trent Water Authority, Malvern, U.K.*). The authors have established that losses from coniferous forested areas exceed those from grassland, the extent of the disparity in drought years depending on the frequency of interception wetting and on soil moisture availability for evaporation. They have also established that dry weather flow yields are a maximum from areas of peat cover.

If forests are planted on peat, infiltration opportunity is increased, subject to interception losses, as root exploitation of the peat layer is more complete and the surface runoff effects associated with grassland are also reduced. Thus, the soil moisture reservoir becomes more flexible, potentially *increasing* the low flow yield during subsequent dry weather.

Do the authors have any evidence that dry weather low yields from forest-covered peat exceed those from grass-covered peat?

R. T. CLARKE AND M. D. NEWSON. We have insufficient evidence to answer Mr Goodhew's question; the minimum flow (per unit area) from the Severn (forested) catchment in 1976 was greater than the minimum flow from the Wye (hill pasture), but this comparison takes no account of the contribution to Severn flow from the unforested peat hags in its headwaters. If, after adjustment for this contribution, the Severn low flow remained greater, it would still be invalid to draw the conclusion that 'trees are better than grass because low flows from forested catchments are higher'; the counter-argument is as given in §4 of our paper which discusses the possible effects of the greater water loss from the forest, during two periods, on decisions taken when planning to meet water demands in subsequent drought periods.

E. B. WORTHINGTON (*I.B.P. Publications Committee, c/o The Linnean Society, London, U.K.*). Have different kinds of grass cover been considered in the work on research catchments? Evaporation from a grass sward closely cropped by sheep must surely be quite different from undergrazed grassland or from grass leys undergoing rapid growth.

R. T. CLARKE AND M. D. NEWSON. The grass cover of the Wye catchment on Plynlimon is composed of 36 % *Nardus/Festuca*, 28 % *Molina* and *Juncus* mires, 26 % old improved pastures with *Agrostis* and clovers, and 10 % heath species such as *Trichophorum* and *Calluna*; it is probably representative of grassland catchments in upland Wales, although in the north of England and Scotland heath species will be more abundant. However, the old improved pastures of the Wye differ in composition and management practice from new mixtures currently recommended for use in mid-Wales; for example tile drainage, which is a prerequisite for the planting of new mixtures, was not a practice with the old pastures of the Wye. As part of an investigation into the removal, by rapid runoff, of fertilizer applied to those mixtures now recommended for planting in upland Wales, the Institute has established two 'natural' lysimeters (one of which is drained and seeded with a new mixture, the other is a control) from which water yields and their quality will be determined in the future; at present, however, we cannot answer the question from experimental results.

W. L. JACK (*Welsh Water Authority, Cambrian Way, Brecon, Powys, U.K.*). At the Welsh Water Authority we are very interested in the Plynlimon results because of their effects on land use in reservoired catchments. However, other workers report no change in water yield due to afforestation. For instance, at the Woodburn catchment in Northern Ireland similar studies were carried out on a grazed area and a forested area, with no similar effect due to trees. As a Water Authority we would not wish to change our land use merely because one scientist has a better publicity agent than another. Can the authors comment on the disparity between their results and those of others working in the same field?

R. T. CLARKE AND M. D. NEWSON. Mr Jack rightly points out that results from other studies, and in particular from the Woodburn catchment in Northern Ireland, appear to conflict with the estimates of water use by forests found at Plynlimon. There are two points that we would make here. The first is specific to the Woodburn study; Savill & Weatherup (1975) were at pains to emphasize the shortcomings of the study. In particular, their pasture catchment contained a high percentage (62 %) of permeable brown earths, and it appears probable that there were unaccounted losses by deep percolation from that catchment. The basis for this statement is that the 12 year mean annual loss (rainfall – runoff) for the pasture catchment is 719 ± 29 mm, while the authors estimate that the annual evaporation is 'unlikely to be less than 400 mm' (the 6 year mean Penman E_T for the Wye catchment, by comparison, is 442 ± 12 mm, with mean annual loss for that catchment of 431 ± 21 mm). For the Woodburn catchment, therefore, assuming an annual E_T of 400 mm, the observed mean annual loss from the pasture catchment is about 80 % greater than E_T for grass; such a large figure is improbable unless there is some unexplained loss from the Woodburn pasture. Savill & Weatherup nevertheless considered that the small pasture catchment was more reliable than the forested catchment, of which they wrote 'there is therefore a strong possibility that large quantities of water were coming into the forest catchment unrecorded from neighbouring land and finding their way out via the flow recorders'. Conclusions about the relative water use of forest and pasture from the Woodburn study must therefore be open to doubt.

Our second point is a more general one. Our colleagues at the Institute, in collaboration with Dr Thom, have shown how the apparently conflicting results from many catchment studies on the water use by trees and grass may be satisfactorily resolved. It is certainly true that trees may not always use more water than grass; in a pine forest in Thetford Chase, Norfolk, for example, our colleagues' studies have shown that the total annual loss from interception and transpiration is 566 mm: lower than the E_T estimate of 643 mm, and suggesting that the annual loss is less than that for grassland. An explanation lies in the rainfall pattern for that region. The forest canopy, compared with that at Plynlimon, is wetted relatively infrequently, although the rate of loss of interception water is high when the canopy is wet; during dry intervals, the pine trees transpire at a rate lower than that from grass under similar climatic conditions. This in no way conflicts with the conclusion that in upland areas, where rainfall is frequent and heavy and from where water supplies are often drawn, interception losses are large because the frequency of canopy wetting is greater.

Reference

Savill, P. S. & Weatherup, S. T. C. 1975 *Forestry* **47**, 45–56.

Proc. R. Soc. Lond. A. **363**, 43–54 (1978)

Printed in Great Britain

The effect of the drought on British agriculture

By E. S. Carter

Agricultural Development and Advisory Service, Ministry of Agriculture, Fisheries and Food, Great Westminster House, Horseferry Road, London SW1P 2AE, U.K.

The drought was most severe in the south of the country, but had serious effects in all areas. The dry summer of 1975 followed by an unusually dry winter resulted in the majority of the country having a soil moisture deficit in May 1976.

Crop production was affected both directly and indirectly through the build up of certain pests and diseases favoured by the weather. Grassland production was severely restricted and some young leys killed out. Livestock remained remarkably fit, but milk yields fell and lambs and grazing cattle took longer to fatten. Supplementary feeding of hay, straw and concentrates was necessary.

Some cases of poisoning resulted from stock foraging for food where pasture was bare, and poor quality water supplies caused problems. There were losses of sheep, pigs and calves due to high temperatures.

Longer term effects of the drought include an enhanced persistence of soil acting herbicides and residues.

THE SEVERITY OF THE DROUGHT

From May 1975 until September 1976 the weather pattern over the British Isles was dominated by high pressure that kept most of the country in a dry situation, although extreme northern areas received a fairly strong southwesterly air flow that accounted for the higher spring rainfall in these parts. The year 1975 proved to be the fifth driest of the century with less than 70 % of the 1916–50 average rainfall from Devon to Yorkshire and in the east of Scotland. South Yorkshire had the driest year since before 1852. Apart from some northern areas that had 150 % of average rainfall, the dry weather continued in February and March 1976 and in the southwest the rainfall deficit was 75 %.

By 1 May 1976 the entire country except the extreme north and parts of north and central Wales were in a state of soil moisture deficit. This was quite severe and in the Midlands deficits of between 75 and 100 mm were recorded at that time. During May there was a little rain in the south and east and significant falls in north England and north Wales. By the beginning of June, soils north of a line from the Humber to the Mersey and including north Wales showed little or no moisture deficit. South of this line the situation was worse than in early May by 20–30 mm.

Exceptionally high temperatures were recorded in June and by the end of the month the main arable areas were showing potential soil moisture deficits well in excess of 100 mm and all other areas were in deficit to a significant extent. By the beginning of August the whole country showed over 100 mm deficit, with 125 mm or over in most of the arable areas.

Between 1 March and 25 August the accumulated potential soil moisture deficit in the south was over 300 mm and in the worst affected areas up to 400 mm. In the north during the same period the soil moisture deficit was less than 300 mm. The drought broke in the last week of August, but rainfall was less in the north and the effects of the dry weather persisted there for 2 or 3 weeks longer than in the south.

CEREAL CROPS

The 1975 harvest was early and gathered quickly; the dry autumn allowed an exceptionally large area of winter wheat and barley to be sown.

In 1976 cereal growth was satisfactory early in the spring, although late frosts were widespread and soil temperatures fell in March. Concern began to be expressed at the end of April about moisture deficits in some soils. Frost damage was widespread in eastern England in early May and by this time cereals in southern England showed signs of moisture stress. By early June winter cereals looked promising, but spring crops in the drier areas were suffering severely from the drought. In northern England conditions were excellent and in mid-June growth was described as 'lush' and fears expressed about the possibility of lodging due to the wet conditions. By the end of June the effects of the hot weather began to appear and spread across the whole country with a serious deterioration in crop prospects. Winter crops died off prematurely and in July the situation got worse and crops deteriorated rapidly. Harvest began in mid-July, the earliest ever recorded, and it was got in quickly and easily. Straw was baled under good conditions. The quality of wheat was good but grain size was poor and shrivelled, and yields below average. Barley was of poor quality with many small pinched grains; yields were small, in some areas virtually a crop failure (table 1).

TABLE 1. CEREAL YIELDS (tonnes per hectare)

	1973	1974	1975	1976	1977 (estimate)
wheat	4.36	4.97	4.34	3.87	4.91
barley	3.97	4.12	3.63	3.57	4.38
oats	3.84	3.77	3.42	3.40	4.36

Regional differences in yield are illustrated in table 2, taking a line from the Severn to the Humber dividing the country into north and south.

Cereal diseases were less serious than usual, barley mildew being the only disease of any significance. The dry conditions impaired the uptake of fungicide and levels of barley mildew (*Erysiphe graminis*) were as high on treated as on untreated crops. Sprays gave a better control than seed treatment. Yellow rust

(*Puccinia striiformis*) and *Septoria* were reported in May and June, but mainly in the north where the drought was less severe. The hot dry weather stopped the development of rusts, *Rhyncosporium*, mildew, *Septoria* and eyespot (*Pseudocercospera herpotrichoides*).

Cereal aphids (*Macrosiphum avenae*) built up to large numbers over a wide area, there were long delays in obtaining aerial spraying contractors and much spraying was done too late to have any real effect.

TABLE 2. REGIONAL DIFFERENCES IN CEREAL YIELD, 1976
(tonnes per hectare)

	north	south
winter wheat	4.14	3.91
spring barley	3.67	3.43

(Data from I.C.I. Recorded Farms)

POTATOES

The 1976 early potato crop was planted in good time and grew well, many crops being irrigated. Lifting took place early, encouraged by high prices, but yields were smaller than in the years before 1975.

The main potato crop was severely affected. Lack of moisture stopped growth and the excessive heat promoted profound physiological effects. Haulm died off during July and August and second growth became widespread, often as chain tuberization. Irrigated crops gave satisfactory yields, but were still affected by the heat in June. The crop was of poor keeping quality aggravated by the appallingly wet conditions at lifting in the autumn. Yields (table 3) were well down resulting in a further shortage and prices rose leading to considerable consumer resistance.

TABLE 3. POTATO YIELDS (tonnes per hectare)

	1973	1974	1975	1976	1977 (estimate)
early	20.1	18.8	14.1	16.3	17.9
maincrop	30.4	31.6	22.3	20.6	30.7

Virus diseases associated with poor quality seed and heavy and early aphid (*Myzus persicae*) infestations connected with the high temperatures caused problems. The dry warm weather favoured cutworms (*Noctuidae*) and damage was widespread and severe, as much as 100 % in some crops in eastern England. No blight (*Phytophthera infestans*) occurred except in some irrigated crops and no blight warnings were issued until the end of August.

SUGAR BEET

Yields have been disappointing since 1974 and in that year virus yellows caused damage and reduced yields. Late sowings and a dry season led to poor yields in 1975 in spite of a lower intensity of virus yellows, although sugar contents were satisfactory.

The 1976 sowing season started very early in the second week of March and was completed by mid-April. Germination was uneven and in the cold conditions of April and early May gappy crops developed. Growth was slow early in the season and virtually ceased in July. Plants survived the drought and at the end of

TABLE 4. SUGAR BEET

	1973	1974	1975	1976
yield of roots (t/ha)	38.4	23.6	24.7	30.7
sugar (%)	15.8	15.5	16.0	14.5
yield of sugar (t/ha)	6.1	3.6	3.9	4.4

August crops were a poor size with high sugar content. Rain in September and October allowed considerable crop growth before harvest, but sugar decreased greatly. Harvesting took place under wet conditions and the campaign was long with some crops lost and subsequently fed to livestock (table 4).

HORTICULTURE

The drought caused a severe reduction in vegetable and fruit supplies and the effects of this continued to be felt well into 1977. Many crops failed and supplies from those that survived were often of very poor quality. Apples yielded near to the average and the quality was good, although small in size and subject to cracking. Soft fruit yielded about 80 % of normal. Field vegetables yielded poorly, probably averaging about 75 % of normal. These estimates cover very wide fluctuations and are affected by irrigation and local conditions. The shortage of vegetables was widespread in Europe so that prices in this country were high and those having crops to sell were not always badly affected financially by the dry weather. One interesting side effect is that during the hot weather it was difficult to obtain casual workers for glasshouse holdings because of the extreme heat.

GRASSLAND

Grassland production was severely restricted in 1976 as it was during the summer of 1975. Cold conditions in April and early May 1976 retarded growth, but during the next 3–4 weeks until mid-June, growth was excellent particularly in the north and Midlands. Adequate grazing was available in May and early June and useful cuts of silage and hay were taken, but regrowth was poor. During the rest of June and July grass growth slowed and eventually ceased altogether. There was some death of grass especially in young leys. It is not easy to measure grassland production as so much is processed through livestock, but some indication can be obtained from estimates of the production of hay (table 5). An estimated 90 % of the crop was of prime or average quality in 1976.

TABLE 5. TOTAL HAY PRODUCTION (kilotonnes)

	1973	1974	1975	1976
temporary grass	3223	2790	2393	2928
permanent grass	3857	3223	2844	3510

FODDER CROPS

Crops grown for forage – kale, mangolds, turnips, swedes – make an important contribution to livestock feeding and in times when hay and silage may be in short supply are regarded as useful substitutes. In 1976 all fodder crops were very severely affected by the drought. They were sown into dry conditions and made virtually no growth at all until the rains came at the end of August. No records are available for the yield of kale, but it is possible to give some indication of the effects of the drought by reference to the estimated yields for the main fodder root crops (table 6).

TABLE 6. FODDER CROPS (tonnes per hectare)

	1973	1974	1975	1976
turnips and swedes	50.7	53.0	46.7	33.2
mangolds	70.5	66.0	59.5	54.3

LIVESTOCK

Grazing livestock were remarkably fit during the hot dry weather. However, by the end of the summer unless their feed had been heavily supplemented, they were in a very lean condition. Breeding animals lost weight and other livestock made small gains in live weight. The most severe effects were seen in dairy herds and milk yields fell very sharply in July and August, not recovering until the autumn. The sales of liquid milk from farms showed a severe drop in production in July, August and September with a compensation later in the year (table 7).

There was heavy supplementary feeding of hay, straw and concentrates all over the country during July and August. Table 8 shows the estimated use in the U.K. of concentrate feed during the past 4 years and shows the substantial increase of imported feed in 1976/77. The true position is emphasized by the fact that since 1974 livestock numbers have fallen by approximately 200000 adult cattle, 500000 pigs, 200000 sheep and some $3\frac{1}{2}$ million poultry. So, fewer livestock consumed a considerable extra quantity of feed. An illustration of the cost of this supplementary feeding may be obtained from Bridgets Experimental Husbandry Farm, Hampshire, where the milk yield decreased by an estimated 270 l per cow and supplementary feeding was necessary at the rate of 150 kg per cow. The net effect of this on a herd of 250 cows was a loss of income of £8500.

TABLE 7. SALES OF LIQUID MILK OFF FARMS (megalitres)

month	1974/75	1975/76	1976/77	% change 1975/76 to 1976/77
April	1019	949	1086	+ 14.5
May	1172	1145	1237	+ 8.0
June	1075	1054	1093	+ 3.7
July	985	951	925	− 2.7
August	919	885	826	− 6.7
September	860	830	778	− 6.3
October	865	886	897	+ 1.3
November	808	871	886	+ 1.7
December	843	904	912	+ 0.9
January	861	922	925	+ 0.4
February	796	875	868	− 1.0
March	914	987	1017	+ 3.0
	11117	**11259**	**11450**	**+1.7**

Data from the Milk Marketing Board.

TABLE 8. USE OF CONCENTRATED FEEDINGSTUFFS (megatonnes)

	1973/74	1974/75	1975/76	1976/77
home grown	14.1	14.0	12.3	12.1
imported	4.7	4.3	5.4	6.6
total	**18.8**	**18.3**	**17.7**	**18.7**

Difficulties naturally arose through shortage of water and in some places although water was available, there was insufficient drinking space because of increased demand. Under these conditions extra trough space would need to be supplied. In one case a dairy herd with an average milk yield of 23 l per cow per day was drinking about 63.5 l of water per cow per day. At peak periods of demand some of the drinking troughs ran dry leading to restlessness on the part of the cows and a drop in yield. It would seem necessary that under these conditions enough drinking trough space should be provided to enable one-tenth of the herd to drink at the same time. There is a distinct social order in dairy herds and cows at the lower end of the social scale may be pushed out of the way and thus go thirsty.

The dry weather had some beneficial effects and parasitic gastro-enteritis in cattle was very mild during the summer grazing period although owing to the late translation of larvae on to the herbage when the wet weather came, there was an increased incidence of this problem during the early winter months of 1977. Salmonellosis was reported as being of slight incidence in June, again possibly associated with the dry weather. A quite common problem during July, August and September was the poisoning of grazing stock attributed to various substances such as lead, arsenic, nitrates and certain weeds. Some of these poisoning incidents were directly attributable to the bare pastures and stock foraging in hedge bottoms for food while others were due to a failure of the water supply and the use of unsatisfactory secondary supplies.

There was some evidence that eye diseases of cattle were more prevalent, probably owing to the activity of flies and to dusty conditions.

Injuries to cows were reported in some areas of the Midlands where the dry weather had resulted in a polishing and hardening of hooves with the result that cattle slipped on dry surfaces, causing bruising and in some cases broken legs.

As with dairy herds, beef cattle at pasture had to receive supplementary feeds of hay and straw and extra amounts of concentrates. Even so, generally there was less liveweight gain. Weaned calves at the Redesdale Experimental Husbandry Farm, Northumberland, were 25 kg below their normal weight when sold in September, and at Rosemaund Experimental Husbandry Farm, Hereford, 18 month old cattle were sold fat at 40 kg below their normal weight in spite of considerable supplementary feed. At Trawsgoed Experimental Husbandry Farm, Aberystwyth, cattle performed quite well in spite of the drought. At High Mowthorpe Experimental Husbandry Farm, North Yorkshire, a very substantial reduction in liveweight gain at grass was compensated during the winter and the animals started to fatten out only a week later than in previous years. Reports of blackleg in cattle were reported to be associated with the ingestion of soil where the stock were on bare pasture.

Generally speaking, sheep remained in very good condition during the hot weather and little effect on ewe performance was noted. However, lambs either took a little longer to fatten or were marginally lighter at slaughter. A reduction of 1.5–2 % in the killing out percentage was reported from several farms recording sheep weights.

An absolute deprivation of water was reported to be responsible for losses of sheep in parts of the north. This occurred on open moorland, water carting being delayed until it was too late.

PIGS AND POULTRY

The effects of the season on pigs and poultry were due to the heat and not the direct effect of the drought. There were outbreaks of 'acute stress syndrome' in pigs particularly during loading. Pigs are, of course, notoriously liable to heatstroke being only sparsely covered with hair and they have inadequate protection from the sun's rays. Wild pigs would wallow in water or mud to cool themselves and under drought conditions water sprays or the provision of shade may be the only alternative to wallowing. In one 2000 sow unit out at grass 50 died on a single very hot day in 1976.

Pasteurellosis in turkeys was responsible for a 2 % fatality due to poor ventilation during the hot conditions.

General effects

Fire damage was quite severe in certain localities. Hedges were burned in many parts of the country, especially beside roads; it was evident that farmers were acutely aware of the fire hazard and many baled their straw rather than risk the dangers of fire from burning. The most serious damage occurred on common land and grazings and other large scrubland areas. There were particularly severe outbreaks in Wales and the heathlands in southern England. In one part of Wales near Corwen, Clywd, about 1250 ha of sheep grazing were destroyed together with many miles of fencing. The cost of restoration will be very high and in some places it is likely to be many years before the area is returned to a reasonable level of production.

Newly planted hedges and woodland suffered badly and a large proportion of the plants died. In Devon a number of hedgerow trees, especially those growing on field banks, were dying in 1977 from the effects of the 1976 drought. It would appear that some of the field banks collapsed because of the combined effects of the drought and the heavy subsequent rainfall. Severe damage was caused to roads in the Fen country with extensive cracking of the surface. Although some buildings in towns were affected by subsidence, this does not appear to have occurred widely with agricultural buildings.

Carting of water was necessary to farms in parts of southwest England and south Wales, and Milk Marketing Board lorries were brought in to help. There were problems of large concentrations of chloride in natural supplies of drinking water caused by saline water backing into drainage channels from elevated waterways with open access to the sea. Some deaths of stock due to salt poisoning were reported.

There was an aggravation of the effects of pests when crops were under drought stress: for example, red spider mite (*Tetranychus urticae*) damage on fruit was unusually severe in the east and, in general, frit fly (*Oscinella frit*) damage was bad in cereal crops where the preceding grassland had been ploughed late in order to conserve forage.

There is a good deal of evidence that the drought lessened the effectiveness of insecticides: for example, brassica seed treatments were less effective against flea beetles (*Crepidodera*) than usual. Granular insecticides were generally ineffective. Cabbage aphid (*Brevicoryne brassicae*) was widespread and control by systemic insecticides was poor in all areas where treatment was considered necessary. Granules were ineffective against cabbage root fly (*Erioischia brassicae*) in all areas apart from northern England where attacks were no more severe than usual.

There was some slight increase in the number of infestations of stored grain by such unusual species as the rice weevil (*Sitophilus oryzae*) that require higher than normal temperatures.

Any soil defects restricting root development – for example cultivation pans – severely affected crops by accentuating moisture stress during the hot weather. The drought also showed up numerous previously unnoticed differences in soil depth and the available water capacity of the subsoil. Heavier soils developed wide and very deep cracks.

There was an increase in the occurrence of nutrient disorders, and deficiencies of potassium in barley, boron in root crops, molybdenum in brassicae, copper in cereals, and manganese in quite a wide range of crops were common. There was reduced uptake of nitrogen and late applications of nitrogenous fertilizers tended to be ineffective. This led to large residues of nitrate in the soil, confirmed by analysis after harvest. After rainfall, abnormally large concentrations of nitrate occurred in some crops, causing poisoning in cattle consuming them. Six dry cows suffered in this way after eating kale, and one Veterinary Investigation Centre found nitrate contents up to $20\,000$ parts/10^6 where 1000 parts/10^6 is considered to be dangerous. Poisoning of a similar nature was also associated with hay and barley straw. Restricted calcium uptake brought about disorders of horticultural crops, such as internal browning in Brussels sprouts and cabbage, and tipburn in lettuce. Fruit crops were also affected: the drought caused premature leaf drop and very small fruit with severe skin cracking and russetting of apples. The autumn rains after the dry weather resulted in a rapid swelling of fruit with a low calcium concentration and poor storage qualities.

THE AFTER-EFFECTS

In general, recovery from the drought was very rapid, with a remarkable change from an arid, burnt-up countryside to green pastures. Unfortunately, the continuous rain during the autumn brought about severe waterlogging and in places where root crops were harvested, damage was caused to the soil structure through traffic in adverse conditions. In those places where large cracks appeared in the soil it would appear that much of the winter rain was lost down these cracks and in the southwest in the spring of 1977, when top soils dried out again, the cracks were revealed as still being present. Such cracking has a long-term beneficial effect on land drainage. In the southwest, hard cloddy soils led to rather poor maize growth in the spring of 1977, and in some fields partial barley failure was attributed to soil impaction caused by lifting potatoes in the wet autumn of 1976. Compaction also occurred in grazing fields due to the pressure on grazing when the grassland had recovered after the drought.

The extended drought resulted in an enhanced persistence of soil-acting herbicides which affected some succeeding crops. In the late summer the residue concentrations were large, and ploughing was advised as recommended by the manufacturers. Unfortunately, farmers were not always prepared to follow the advice. Because of the 1975 summer drought and the small 1975/76 winter rainfall, residues of some herbicides were more persistent and there were several cases of early damage to winter cereals.

In those areas where the drought was severe, particularly the southwest, grassland appeared to suffer very severely, although with the onset of rain at the end of August recovery was rapid and spectacular and the grass became green in a few days. It would seem that perennial ryegrass-dominant swards made a very full recovery and the only loss of plant was recorded on thin soils on south facing slopes where they were particularly severely affected by the dry weather. Other types of permanent grass containing *Agrostis* species and Yorkshire Fog (*Holcus lanatus*) and a large proportion of broad-leaved weeds made a good recovery, but there would appear to have been an increase in broad leaved weeds at the expense of the weed grasses. Italian ryegrass leys were the most vulnerable and suffered the greatest loss of plant, particularly those that were sown in 1974. Very heavy losses of leys undersown in 1976 were recorded, but perhaps surprisingly the seed from some leys sown in April remained dormant throughout the drought period and gave a good germination in September when the rain came.

Among individual grass species, perennial ryegrass, cocksfoot, timothy and tall fescue all made a full recovery and meadow fescue suffered the greatest loss. The tetraploid varieties of ryegrass remained green during the drought but produced very little in the way of grazing and the same was true of cocksfoot and tall fescue. Lucerne alone of all the herbage species made active growth during the drought owing to its drought resistant characteristics.

The wet spring conditions in 1976 resulted in good quantities of first cut silage, but the quality was slightly lower than in the previous year although better than the long term average. Hay crops were made in excellent weather, but the fall in digestibility during June was more rapid than usual and the final quality of the hay was not quite as good as in 1975. After the drought there was a tendency to overestimate the value of the flush of grass and some herds lost body condition. By the end of 1976 problems of poorly sustained milk yields and low solids-not-fat were becoming apparent in those herds that had not overcome the effects of the drought so successfully. Problems of acidosis, ketosis and low butterfat content were associated with feeding diets containing only restricted quantities of fodder. The drought appeared to result in increased crude protein contents of cereal grains, and samples of high crude protein barley and wheat indicated that the quality of the protein from the 1976 cereal harvest was higher than normally expected. The metabolizable energy value of barley was about 5 % less than normal.

Owing to the shortage of supplies of fodder, there was concern for the feeding position during the 1976/77 winter. A good deal of straw was baled, and advisers received enquiries about methods of conservation and the utilization of unusual feeds, such as carrot tops, potato peelings, cauliflower and celery waste. There was also an increased interest in the production and utilization of straw treated with sodium hydroxide. There is no doubt that in general farmers having sought advice made the best possible use of their limited supplies of conserved forages.

In some parts of the country the effects of the extreme drought led to the failure of some drainage systems during the later period of heavy rain. Deep penetration of roots searching for moisture had completely blocked drains, sometimes of quite a large diameter; this involved kale as well as hedge roots. In other places mole channels became filled with fine soil washed down by the heavy rain through fissures enlarged during the drought.

The drought naturally affected British agriculture: both by the direct effect of lack of moisture, resulting in stress conditions for growing crops and for livestock, and by the very high temperatures. As this country does not rely entirely on its own resources to feed its livestock, farmers were able, at a cost, to draw on outside supplies to compensate for failure of home-grown feeds. There was a drop in livestock production, particularly with grazing animals, and a fall in the yield of crops. The consumer felt the effect of this in higher prices as it was not always possible to compensate by imports owing to similar conditions in Europe or a shortage of a particular commodity in the world at large. There was a remarkably quick recovery when the rains came. Pastures greened up rapidly and seeds sown under dry conditions germinated giving quite reasonable forage and other crops. During the summer and in the autumn many farmers were interested in increased water storage facilities so that they could practise at least limited irrigation in the case of another drought and increased rates of grant were offered in 1977. Over 400 applications have been made for the higher grant, but only a small proportion of this work has been completed so far.

The Meteorological Office claim that such a season was one in 500 years: let us hope they are right.

Discussion

E. B. WORTHINGTON (*I.B.P. Publications Committee, c/o The Linnean Society, London, U.K.*). Have delayed effects of the drought, already noted in the cases of tree death and the persistent effect of insecticides and herbicides, been recorded in the physiology of domestic animals? For example, dairy farmers in Sussex have, during 1977, experienced unusual difficulty in the stocking of cows through artificial insemination, and were inclined to attribute this to nutritional deficiencies experienced during the drought.

E. S. CARTER. No adverse effects on conception rates to artificial insemination were recorded during the 1975–76 drought. There was a slight improvement of conception rates at the end of the 1976 summer thought to be associated with a better relative nutritional status resulting from feeding extra hay and concentrates at a time when milk yields were decreasing due to drought effects.

B. RYDZ (6, *Kingsdown House, Box, Corsham, Wiltshire, SN14 9AX, U.K.*). I should like to mention a problem to which attention has been drawn since the early 1960s arising out of the licensing provisions of the 1963 Water Resources Act.

Since that time and, particularly during the wet summers of the late 1960s, the enthusiasm of farmers for providing their own irrigation storage seems to have waned. It is right that they should be the judges of this, although in some regions the incidence of abstraction charges for filling farm storage might usefully be reviewed.

There are a few areas, however, where it might be economic for the water authorities to make capital investments to support supplies for irrigation (for instance, in parts of the Warwickshire Avon catchment) provided they could be reasonably sure of recovering licence revenue to meet capital charges. But, at present, it is possible for farmers to surrender their licences and apply for renewal at any time whereas the water authority can only revoke a licence with liability for payment of compensation. In these circumstances not much is likely to be spent to support a sporadic demand like that for irrigation unless provision is made for long-term contracts with farmers or, perhaps, farming cooperatives.

Such contracts occur in more established irrigation economies overseas; and the requisitioning procedure applicable to certain other water services under the 1973 Water Act could perhaps be adapted for the purpose.

If the M.A.F.F. is concerned to see opportunities for this kind of investment more seriously examined, they might well take some initiative in this matter.

E. S. CARTER. Since the meeting I have taken this matter up with the appropriate division in M.A.F.F. who are examining the proposal in consultation with the other interested Government Departments.

Proc. R. Soc. Lond. A. **363**, 55–68 (1978)

Printed in Great Britain

The effects of the 1975–76 drought on groundwater and aquifers

By J. B. W. Day† and J. C. Rodda‡

† *Hydrogeology Unit, Institute of Geological Sciences,*
Exhibition Road, South Kensington, London SW7 2DE, U.K.
‡ *Water Data Unit, Department of the Environment,*
Reading Bridge House, Reading RG1 8PS, U.K.

The drought of 1975–76 that affected not only the British Isles but extended to much of the continent of Europe, became severe only after the exceptionally dry winter of 1975/76 when within most of England and Wales negligible recharge to aquifers occurred. Thus by the spring of 1976 when seasonal underground storage should have been at its peak, aquifer storage was already at a very low level. Since, however, groundwater levels in aquifers are controlled by local and variable base level drainage conditions, the extent to which further falls in level could occur under natural unconfined conditions was limited so that by autumn 1976 in most places levels were lower than those previously recorded by only a few metres. Within confined aquifers having lower storativities, effects were usually more severe and falls in level below those previously recorded of more than 10 m occurred. Had it not been for the exceptionally wet winter of 1974/75 when recharge to aquifers was generally well above average, groundwater levels in the autumn of 1976 might have been considerably lower.

The authors have been unable to discern any long-term adverse effects on British aquifers in which by the early spring of 1977 groundwater levels had, in almost every known case, recovered to higher than average levels except in areas with levels lowered previously by over-abstraction.

No permanent ill effects on groundwater quality have so far become apparent.

1. Introduction

The hydrometeorological definition of an absolute drought most commonly used in Britain is 15 consecutive days to none of which is credited 0.25 mm or more of rainfall. If hydrogeologists were to apply a similar definition to that proportion of rainfall which penetrates the soil zone to recharge the aquifers beneath, 'infiltration droughts' would be annual, prolonged and wholly predictable. Many experienced hydrogeologists therefore took a fairly relaxed view of the 1975–76 drought which, in infiltration terms, although of much greater duration than its recent predecessors, they regarded as differing essentially in degree only. For it is a fact that in the absence of abstraction the effects on major aquifers and the bulk of their stored groundwaters of an 18 month 'infiltration drought' – three times the normal summer period – are, in the context of total groundwater

[55]

storage, little more severe than those to be expected after a single more normal summer.

This sweeping statement demands explanation, but it must first be pointed out that the abnormal reduction in groundwater levels and storage that occurred during 1976, although slight in overall terms, was nevertheless critical to the maintenance of groundwater supplies from wells and boreholes, the depths and pump settings of which were designed to meet more normal circumstances.

Groundwater makes a significant contribution to water supplies within England and Wales: during 1975, one-third of the water used for public supply came from groundwater sources (Anon. 1976a). In some areas, particularly in southern and eastern England, this proportion is considerably higher. The Chalk and the Triassic sandstones are the most important British aquifers.

Within Britain, rainfall on average is evenly distributed between the summer and winter. By far the greater part of all evaporation (including transpiration) occurs during the period April–September to an extent that mostly precludes significant water movement below the soil layers. By contrast, most of the rainfall during the months of October to March, after satisfying soil moisture deficits, either drains from the surface into rivers or passes through permeable strata as recharge to aquifers. Under unconfined conditions infiltrating water passes vertically downwards through an unsaturated zone to the deeper saturated zone interfaced by the water table which, subject to atmospheric pressure, fluctuates in response to the ratio recharge:discharge, rising when the former exceeds the latter and vice versa. In fine grained fissured aquifers such as the Chalk, with low specific yields commonly within the range of 1–5 %, seasonal water table fluctuations at sites remote from natural discharges can exceed 30 m. Comparable fluctuations in Triassic sandstones, which have much higher specific yields (commonly within the range 20–25 %) are much less, 5 m being a typical maximum. Peak levels and thus maximum storage are normally attained in late winter or early spring receding to a minimum in late autumn, by which time the rate of fall of level is much reduced. The form of the Chilgrove well hydrograph (figure 1) for 1974 is fairly typical. With the onset of winter rainfall, the cycle is repeated, but if a dry winter results in negligible infiltration, there is little or no concomitant rise in levels which then continue to fall throughout the winter but at a much reduced rate.

This slow fall is continued during the following summer if there is no rainfall of sufficient magnitude to cause infiltration. Thus, by the end of the period, levels and storage are likely to be appreciably, but not excessively, lower than they were the previous autumn. Generally speaking, this is what happened during the summer and intervening winter of 1975–76.

When groundwater levels are highest, normally in spring, so are natural discharges from springs in response to the increased hydraulic gradients. As levels recede, so do discharges which also reach minima in autumn. Cessation of spring discharge rarely indicates complete draining of its contributory aquifer, more commonly a lessening of gradients in response to natural or artificial drainage possibly from a lower level elsewhere.

Aquifer storage is commonly described as 'temporary' or 'permanent'. The former refers to water stored between the highest and lowest levels of the water table and thus subject to seasonal drainage, which, averaged over a long period, itself provides a measure of the average recharge. However, below the minimum level of the water table in major aquifers lies a great volume of saturated rock that provides permanent storage available to wells of adequate depth but which cannot be drained naturally. In the absence of winter infiltration this permanent storage remains, but, because there is no normal rise in levels and hence seasonal storage, springs and the dependent base flows of rivers suffer.

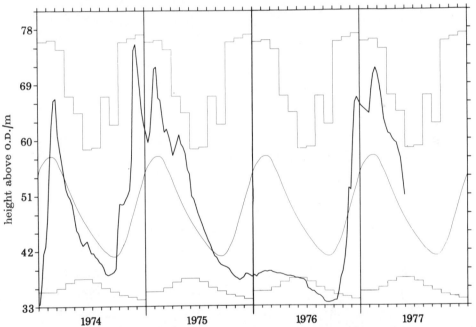

FIGURE 1. Well hydrograph for Chilgrove House, Chilgrove (National Grid Reference SU 835 144), based on weekly readings. Hydrometric area 41; aquifer, Chalk; surface level 77.1 m O.D. Records from 1836 to 1973 were used to produce the maximum, minimum and average values.

Over large areas of Britain's main aquifer, the Chalk, the potential ratio of 'permanent' to 'temporary' storage may be of the order 10:1, but the proportion is not a simple thickness relation.

2. OVERTURE TO THE DROUGHT

Over the country as a whole, rainfall was markedly below average throughout the period 1971–74. By December 1973 levels in the Chalk well at Chilgrove, Sussex, for which regular records have been kept since 1836 (Thomson 1938) had fallen below the long-term average minimum for the month, although in the Chalk of North Norfolk and Humberside, levels more nearly approached the average. Recharge during the winter of 1973–74 did not commence until January in a number of areas and the start of 1974, like 1973, saw water tables at levels that were below or considerably below average. However, rainfall during the winter of 1974–75 was generally above average and sufficient to cause water tables to attain average or above average levels in most areas. The spring commenced with British aquifers well stocked. In the Chilgrove well three peaks were recorded, in November, February and April, and similar, although more subdued, patterns were discernable in the more northerly Chalk wells. On Humberside substantial recharge occurred as late as April/May.

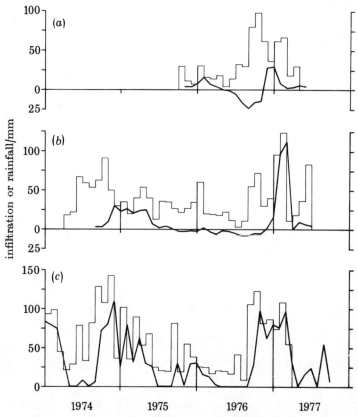

FIGURE 2. Infiltration (curve) and rainfall (histogram) for three lysimeter sites: (a) Reach, Cambs.; (b) Styrrup, Notts.; (c) Rothamsted, Herts. Negative infiltration values denote an upward moisture flux within the lysimeter.

The volume of water reaching the saturated zone can be measured by lysimeters (Kitching & Bridge 1974) and by tensiometric methods (Anon. 1976b) and it may also be estimated from measurement of other variables such as rainfall. However, direct measurements are not simple to make and there is a degree of uncertainty about estimates. Figure 2 shows measurements of infiltration, compared with local rainfall, at three lysimeter sites, mostly for the period January 1974 to June 1977. The lysimeters at Styrrup (Kitching & Bridge 1974) and Reach are large with undisturbed cores and a water table maintained at natural levels, while those at Rothamsted are much smaller, less deep, without a saturated zone and carry no crop. The results from Styrrup clearly show substantial infiltration during the winters of 1974/75 and 1976/77 and its almost complete absence during the period June 1975 to November 1976. However, the record at Reach, which started in October 1975, shows some infiltration during the ensuing winter months.

There is no doubt that the greatly increased storage in aquifers represented by high water levels experienced throughout the winter of 1974 and most importantly during the spring of 1975 sustained groundwater levels (by markedly delaying the onset of recession of levels due to drainage) and hence spring flows during the ensuing long dry periods. This wet winter more than made up for the cumulative effects of the previous cycle of dry years; had it not occurred the groundwater supply situation during the final months of the ensuing 'great drought' could have been a good deal more serious than it in fact was.

3. THE DROUGHT

Although this symposium and this paper are solely concerned with the scientific effect of the drought within England and Wales, it should be remembered that a large part of western Europe was also affected (Meaden 1976); the effects within the Loire Brittany Basin were particularly severe (Anon. 1976d). However, within Britain, the lack of rainfall that occurred from May 1975 onwards was not reflected in water table levels below average until September over much of the Chalk and also in other aquifers. From that month water levels in some aquifers continued to fall slowly, in some they were more or less stationary, while in others slight rises in levels showed that very small amounts of recharge were taking place. This pattern varied locally but, in general, wells in the southeast, particularly in the Chalk, showed falls in levels, while those further north and west were either stationary or rising slightly. This situation was maintained throughout the winter of 1975/76, a number of well levels falling below the lowest previously recorded for the time of year. For example, at Rockley near Marlborough, record low water levels were registered from the beginning of 1976 until the well went dry during the last week in June. Most levels continued to fall during the spring in the absence of recharge; wells in the southwest were considerably below the lowest recorded for the time of year in the month of April. This pattern of falling water levels was continued in most aquifers through May, June and July as the drought intensified, although in some areas, such as the northeast and the northwest, levels were not as depressed as elsewhere. By August, record low levels were being registered in many wells and a number of dug wells simply dried up. At Chilgrove new minima were recorded for the months of July, August and September. On the other hand, similar extremes were not recorded in regions to the west; for example, in the well in the Great Oolite Series at Westonbirt School, Tetbury, Gloucestershire. In the Lincolnshire Limestone aquifer of the Bourne (Lincolnshire) area, falls in levels of more than 10 m below those previously recorded occurred (Anon. 1977), but the effects of heavy abstraction for public supply under confined (artesian) conditions contributed largely to these exceptional figures.

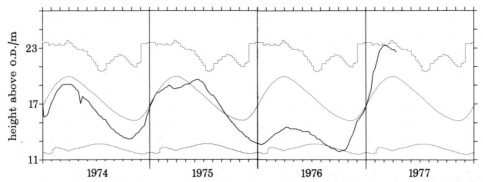

FIGURE 3. Well hydrograph for Dalton Estate, Dalton Holme (National Grid Reference SE 965 453), based on weekly readings. Hydrometric area 26; aquifer, Chalk; surface level 113.4 m O.D. Records from 1889 to 1973 were used to produce the maximum, minimum and average values.

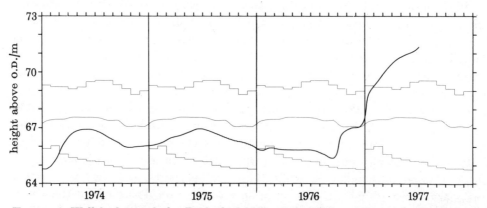

FIGURE 4. Well hydrograph for Rushyford N.E., Great Chilton (National Grid Reference NZ 2875 2896), based on monthly readings. Hydrometric area 25; aquifer, Magnesian Limestone; surface level 92.5 m O.D. Records from 1967 to 1973 were used to produce the maximum, minimum and average values.

It is not intended in this short paper to review comprehensively the minimum groundwater levels recorded because these will be published in detail elsewhere (for instance in *Water Data*) but figure 1 and figures 3–10 show hydrographs for a number of representative wells in major aquifers for the period January 1974 to spring 1977. As far as possible the wells from which the hydrographs have been obtained are thought to have been unaffected by pumping unless otherwise stated, but during a period of drought it is not always possible without detailed analysis readily to distinguish natural effects from the artificial effects of abstraction.

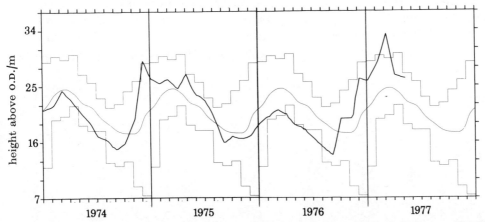

FIGURE 5. Well hydrograph for Chalk Farm, Narborough (National Grid Reference TF 7759 1069), based on weekly readings. Hydrometric area 33; aquifer, Chalk; surface level 48.1 m O.D. Records from 1950 to 1973 were used to produce the maximum, minimum and average values.

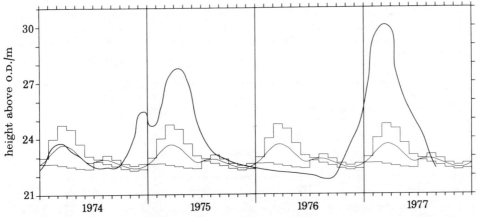

FIGURE 6. Well hydrograph for Careby (National Grid Reference TF 026 155), based on monthly readings. Hydrometric area 31; aquifer, Lincolnshire Limestone; surface level 35.8 m O.D. Records from 1972 to 1973 were used to produce the maximum, minimum and average values.

4. RECOVERY FROM THE DROUGHT

By the end of July 1976 estimated soil moisture deficits exceeded 138 mm over much of the Midlands, south, and east of England (Anon. 1976c) and deficits of this order continued throughout much of August. Thus the effect of the rainfall at the end of August and during September was not to produce an immediate rise in water levels in all wells; some aquifers responded in the second half of September, but in others, particularly the Chalk, well levels continued to fall during September, and it was not until October that the reversal took place. During November, the levels in many wells had reached average or above average, but there were some, e.g. the well in the Chalk at Odsey, Norfolk, where the rise from the summer minimum did not commence until the end of the year or even into 1977. However, by the spring of 1977, on a countrywide basis, groundwater levels were standing above or well above those of the previous four or five years.

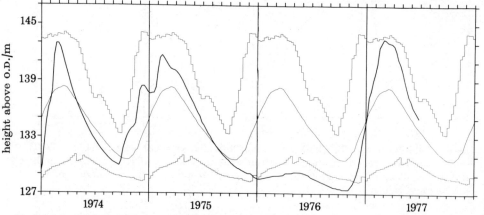

FIGURE 7. Well hydrograph for Rockley, Ogbourne St Andrew (National Grid Reference SU 165 717), based on weekly readings. Hydrometric area 39; aquifer, Chalk; surface level 146.4 m O.D. Records from 1933 to 1973 were used to produce the maximum, minimum and average values.

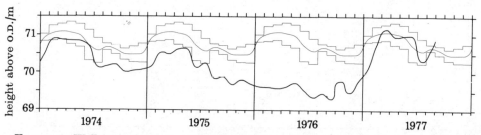

FIGURE 8. Well hydrograph for New House Farm (National Grid Reference SJ 586 234), based on monthly readings. Hydrometric area 54; aquifer, Bunter Sandstone; surface level 74.3 m O.D. Records from 1972 to 1973 were used to produce the maximum, minimum and average values.

5. EFFECTS ON GROUNDWATER AND AQUIFERS

Short-term, physical

By the autumn of 1977 groundwater levels in major aquifers over much of the country were generally lower than previously recorded – albeit mostly by a few metres only – although this was not everywhere the case and it was evident that the effects of the drought were locally variable. However, when hydraulic gradients and drainage by discharge are minimal (as they were then) further falls in levels were likely to be slow and slight. In this condition the effects of artificial abstraction become proportionately greater, and the distance at which effects are noticeable is greatly increased. In an observation well not normally affected by abstraction, such effects are difficult to distinguish but a tendency for the hydrograph when plotted on a natural scale to be convex upwards during a period of no infiltration suggests artificially depleted levels. For instance, the hydrograph of the Chilgrove well for the period May to August 1976 suggests interference, possibly due to

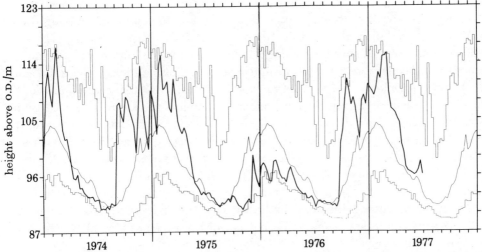

FIGURE 9. Well hydrograph for Westonbirt School, Tetbury (National Grid Reference ST 864 903), based on weekly readings. Hydrometric area 53; aquifer, Great Oolite Series; surface level 120.7 m O.D. Records from 1932 to 1973 were used to produce the maximum, minimum and average values.

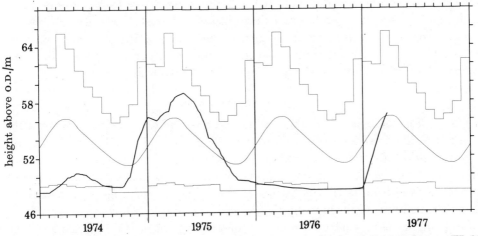

FIGURE 10. Well hydrograph for Odsey, Guilden Morden (National Grid Reference TL 2947 3825), based on weekly readings. Hydrometric area 33; aquifer, Chalk; surface level 78.0 m O.D. Records from 1903 to 1973 were used to produce the maximum, minimum and average values.

pumping. However, rainfall in the south and southeast of England during July was variable in distribution and incidence, the mean being 29.3 mm (47 % of the July long-term average) (Anon. 1976c). Although soil moisture deficits were far greater at this time, some fissure infiltration may have caused slight rises in the well hydrographs within this area.

When hydraulic gradients between catchments and their natural outlets are minimal so are natural discharges; Ineson & Downing (1964) established a direct relation between water levels within a catchment and the discharges therefrom. In some places spring flows may cease altogether, e.g. the springs supplying Ross on Wye (which failed also in the summer of 1973), while in others, e.g. the Bedhampton group of springs forming the main supply for Portsmouth, minimal groundwater levels were reflected in much reduced flows although these did not fall below previously recorded minima (G. Slater, personal communication). The flows of surface streams during prolonged droughts are entirely derived from groundwater seepage, but since this topic is being explored in another paper, only brief reference to it will be made here. Seasonal streams known as 'Winterbournes', 'Nailbournes' or 'Lavants' in Chalk areas are a feature of permeable catchments where the dominant mode of saturated flow within the aquifer is through fissures. The lavant's point of emergence migrates up and down the valley according to the level of the water table, and the lowest point of emergence – the 'perennial head' – marks the intersection of the bottom of the topographic valley with the minimum seasonal level of the water table at that point.

During the winter of 1975/76 most seasonal streams failed to flow over any portion of their courses, and by August/September 1976 many 'perennial heads' were dry, the waters – much diminished – emerging at a new level appropriate to the reduced level of the water table, in some cases several hundreds of metres down stream. Throughout much of the Chalk of the Berkshire Downs groundwater levels were between 2 and 3 m below those previously recorded (M. Owen, personal communication) and the perennial head of the River Kennet receded accordingly. In the cases of other seasonal streams in this area (e.g. the Lambourn and the Pang) the situation was obscured by augmentation pumping.

Short-term, chemical

After a prolonged period of dry weather and high soil temperature it was widely expected that initial infiltration after the drought would flush through the soil large amounts of soluble minerals possibly leading to significant pollution of groundwater. In particular it was expected that there might be serious flushing of nitrates derived from fertilizers. Although there was a sudden marked increase in the nitrate concentrations in many rivers (see, for example, Toms 1977) which later fell to more normal levels, no significant increase was recorded from the majority of wells drawing water from aquifers having an unsaturated zone of appreciable thickness. In almost all cases known to us where sudden deteriorations of ground-water quality were recorded, the sources were either springs or boreholes with access to groundwater derived from shallow depth, either because of natural hydrogeological conditions or because of some fault in the construction of the source. At a research groundwater catchment in Norfolk, continuous monitoring of Chalk groundwater quality at depth beneath arable land failed to detect any appreciable sudden rise in nitrate concentrations when infiltration commenced in February 1977. A slight rise (about 2 mg/l (NO_3)N) in a nearby Chalk public supply source was attributed to shallow groundwater derived from an adjacent ephemeral stream.

We are not aware of any significant long-term effect on groundwater or aquifers which can positively be ascribed to the drought of 1975/76.

6. THE DROUGHT IN PERSPECTIVE

Water resources in England and Wales are already highly developed and the range of options for further development is perhaps somewhat restricted. Similarly, the ways in which water supplies could be augmented during a drought are rather limited. These opinions are in marked contrast to some of the views expressed in the popular press at the height of the recent drought which made it seem as if development of a water grid, or of desalination, or of groundwater to a greater extent than at present, would solve all the country's water supply problems, simply and cheaply. Although groundwater reserves within the uppermost 50 m of the major aquifers are up to two orders of magnitude greater than the total storage in the country's reservoirs (Rodda, Downing & Law 1976) exploitation of these reserves during a drought by deepening existing wells and sinking new ones would be difficult, if not impossible. Cost and limited drilling facilities are obvious problems, but there are others such as a deterioration in quality and a further decrease in the baseflow (groundwater) component of river flow, quite apart from the effects on existing wells. Reduction in yields due to decrease of hydraulic conductivity with lowered water levels is another possible problem, but knowledge of the variations of aquifer characteristics with increasing depth is limited and there is scope for further research in this area. In the regional context perhaps greater emphasis should be put on the conjunctive use of surface and groundwater: schemes to augment river flows from specially constructed well fields show considerable promise. Locally, water can be abstracted from shallow aquifers, such as Glacial Sands and Gravels and other superficial deposits, and used for purposes other than public supply, thereby reducing demand on the public water supply.

Unless quite disproportionate amounts of capital and works are to be continuously sterilized against the statistical improbability of another drought comparable to or worse than that of 1975/76, it seems that we must to a great extent continue to rely on the ingenuity of our hydrologists, hydrogeologists and water engineers and the ability of the Public to tighten its belt.

66   J. B. W. Day and J. C. Rodda (Discussion Meeting)

This paper is published by permission of the Director, Institute of Geological Sciences, and the Director, Water Data Unit of the Department of the Environment. The authors wish to acknowledge the assistance of Mr M. Owen (Thames Water Authority) and Mr G. Slater (Portsmouth Water Company) and the help of Mrs H. Giddings and of Mr M. Lees, Mrs M. Notting and Miss P. Dennison in selecting the well data and preparing the well hydrographs. Thanks are also due to those water authorities whose data were used in preparing this paper. The opinions expressed by the authors are not necessarily those of the Institute of Geological Sciences nor the Department of the Environment.

REFERENCES (Day & Rodda)

Anon. 1976*a* *Water data 1975*. London: H.M.S.O.

Anon. 1976*b* *Research Report 1974–6*. Institute of Hydrology.

Anon. 1976*c* Water Situation Report: July 1976. (Circulated report.) Reading: Central Water Planning Unit.

Anon. 1976*d* The drought in the Loire–Brittany Basin. *T.S.M. L'eau*. October, p. 285.

Anon. 1977 *The 1975–6 drought*. National Water Council.

Ineson, J. & Downing, R. A. 1964 The groundwater component of river discharge and its relationship to hydrogeology. *J. Instn Wat. Engrs* **18**, 519–541.

Kitching, R. & Bridge, L. R. 1974 Lysimeter installations in sandstone at Styrrup, Notts. *J. Hydrol.* **23**, 219–232.

Meaden, G. T. 1976 North West Europe's great drought. *J. Meteorology* I, **12**.

Rodda, J. C., Downing, R. A. & Law, F. M. 1976 *Systematic hydrology*. London: Butterworth.

Thomson, D. H. 1938 A hundred years record of Rainfall and Water levels in the Chalk at Chilgrove, West Sussex. *Trans. Instn Wat. Engrs* **43**, 154–196.

Toms, R. 1977 Scientific aspects and technical innovations. One day *Seminar on the operational aspects of the drought 1975–76* (preprint papers), pp. 3, 1–3, 18. Institution of Water Engineers and Scientists and Institute of Civil Engineers.

Discussion

D. J. Burdon (*Groundwater Division, Geological Survey of Ireland*, 14 *Hume St., Dublin 2, Eire*). In Ireland, in contrast to much of England and Wales, the 36 months beginning with September 1974 were dry, but the below-average precipitation was confined to the summer months, while winter precipitation was close to average. Under these general conditions, groundwater levels and resources fluctuated more or less normally throughout the period. Data from the groundwater observation well at Masterton, Corbally Townland, Stradbally, Co. Laoise (limestone aquifer under gravels), and from the nearby precipitation station at Kilberry (Bord na Mona), Co. Kildare, make more precise this general observation. Comparing precipitation over the 30 year period 1941–70 with precipitation over the 36 months commencing 1 September 1974, it is found that: (i) annual precipitation decreased by 17.7 % from 769 to 633 mm; (ii) winter (7 months to 31 March) precipitation decreased by only 4.5 % from 67 to 64.1 mm per month; but (iii) summer precipitation (5 months) decreased by 38.3 % from 60 to 37 mm per month. The observation well shows an average annual fluctuation in groundwater levels of 7.5 m, with a peak in February and a trough in October–November.

During the 36 months of low precipitation, the well showed rises of 6.0 m (to 12 February 1975), of 5.8 m (to 7 April 1976) and of 9.3 m (to 23 February 1977). Falls were 7.5 m (to 6 October 1975) and 6.6 m (to 22 October 1976), while the lowest point for 1977 does not yet appear to have been reached. These Irish observations (for which I am obliged to my colleague Mr C. R. Aldwell of the Irish Geological Survey and to the Irish Meteorological Service) covering the period of the 1975–76 winter drought in England and Wales provide striking confirmation of the now well established fact that a dry winter will reduce ground-water supplies in the following summer, while a dry summer has little or no effect on the groundwater régime.

With regard to the recognition, so clearly demonstrated in the paper, that the static (or capital) groundwater reserves greatly exceed in volume the dynamic (or annual) resources, I enquire, first, to what extent these static reserves can be brought into use in an emergency such as the 16 month drought, and secondly, what are likely to be the long term effects of such an extraction of the static reserves?

J. B. W. DAY AND J. C. RODDA. We are indebted to Dr Burdon for his comments on the effects – or more strictly, lack of effects – of the drought in Eire. He has provided some valuable data which might otherwise have gone unrecorded in this country.

With regard to Dr Burdon's first question, it is perfectly possible to draw on the 'permanent' groundwater storage during drought conditions, although great care has to be exercised as to how, when and where it is done, otherwise there can be serious effects on existing nearby wells or natural spring discharges.

There are now a number of British schemes to augment river flows periodically in times of drought by pumping from wells remote from springs and discharging via pipelines to the nearest part of the river system that carries perennial flow. When the pumps are started, the net gain to the river is total, but the gain reduces slowly as hydraulic gradients towards natural discharges are affected by pumping. Normally, augmentation wells are pumped during the summer and autumn, and pumping stops when infiltration from winter rainfall restores groundwater levels, gradients and discharges, repaying as it were the temporary overdraft from permanent storage.

However, there may be severe difficulties with those schemes that augment from unconfined aquifers if a dry winter (without significant infiltration) were to follow a period of pumping. After an extended period of pumping – in very general terms about 1 year – net gain would eventually become net loss and from that time until there were sufficient infiltration to restore the situation, local river flow (despite continued augmentation) would be less than it otherwise would have been had pumping not taken place. Stopping the pumps under such conditions would then have catastrophic effects upon the already diminished flows in the river concerned.

In other words, augmentation pumps, once started, must operate until the normal winter rains arrive; without rain, or if there is little resultant infiltration, they must continue to operate all through that winter and most probably the following summer as well. Such would have been the case had an augmentation scheme been started during the summer of 1975; by late summer 1976 the consequences to the flows of the river concerned could have been most serious.

Any possible long-term effects on aquifers of deliberate over-abstraction are likely to be related to the unusual drawdown of water levels in the aquifer concerned and how often it occurs. To the extent that circulation of water at these levels would be enhanced, in the very long term some increase in permeability might be expected as well as chemical changes due to oxidation, mainly along fissures. In our view, such changes, related to a realistic time scale, can be expected to be slight.

In general we strongly support properly planned river augmentation schemes, although we feel that there should be a wider understanding of the potential problems posed by the possibility – admittedly remote – of a recurrence of long-period drought conditions such as those recently experienced.

Proc. R. Soc. Lond. A. **363**, 69–96 (1978)

Printed in Great Britain

The effects of drought on the river systems

By M. J. Hamlin† and C. E. Wright‡

† Department of Water Engineering, University of Birmingham,
P.O. Box 363, Birmingham B15 2TT, U.K.
‡ Central Water Planning Unit, Reading Bridge House,
Reading RG1 8PS, U.K.

The drought of 1975–76 had a significant effect on the river systems of England and Wales and will be used in water resources design for many years. It is therefore important to recognize that for the river flows it was not uniformly severe. Further, for many purposes, the duration of the low flow is at least as important as its severity. As an example, for the river Thames at Teddington it was only for periods of one and two months that the flow in 1976 was lower than that in 1921.

The paper reviews the conditions which give rise to low flows in rivers, compares a representative set of low flow records, comments on criteria which were used to reduce the effect of the drought on the quantity and quality of river flows and suggests methods by which the management of rivers in time of drought might be improved.

Introduction

Droughts in this country have always attracted attention and there are many interesting accounts that describe previous historic shortages. Matthew Paris (1884), in an account of the drought of 1252–53, states 'In this year [1253] there was in the summer a great and prolonged drought, but at the end of the summer and in the autumn, the rivers overflowed their banks and rose to the top of the hills drowning the adjoining places.'

A discussion on the severity of the 1975–76 drought will necessarily include a range of scientific disciplines such as meteorology, agriculture and water resources. Each of these disciplines will define the drought and its severity in terms of the effect on the community in its particular field of interest. In water resources the word 'drought', like the word 'flood', needs to have a probability of occurrence attached to it to give it scientific meaning. In addition the period for which a drought lasts is crucial in assessing the severity of its effect.

Further, the term 'drought' is often used to describe both the shortage of rainfall and the shortage of river flow. Often the severity of one is assumed to be equal to the severity of the other. This is not the case. It does not follow that because the rainfall event has a recurrence interval of once in 500 years – an often quoted figure last year – that the river flow drought will also have a severity of once in 500 years. This misconception led to a number of decisions which were difficult to justify in scientific terms. Nevertheless, the difficulty of defining the

[69]

severity of a river flow drought while the drought continues should not be under-estimated since adequate analysis can only be carried out after the event has ended. During 1976 the problems were essentially operational; today planners are examining the severity of the event.

THE EFFECT OF RAINFALL AND CATCHMENT CHARACTERISTICS ON RUN-OFF

It is not possible to discuss the low flows in any river system without some preliminary thought being given to the mechanisms that give rise to low flows. These may be subdivided into the causal precipitation and the effect of the catchment characteristics, such as soil type, land use, topography, geology and stream patterns. A simple conceptual model, after Dawdy & O'Donnell (1965), is given

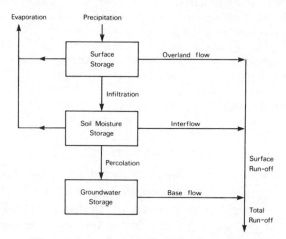

FIGURE 1. A conceptual catchment model.

in figure 1. This model traces the two main routes by which rainfall becomes river flow. However, the time constants for the two components vary very considerably so that a single rainfall event which may have an immediate effect on surface run-off will have a delayed effect on the base flow contribution to run-off. The extent of this delay may be up to 2 or 3 months as it is for the river Elan, up to 7 months for the Severn at Bewdley, or up to 18 months for the Thames at Teddington.

Rainfall

The water available for run-off is primarily a function of precipitation and then a function of the amount lost by evaporation. For as river flow, both the short-term and long-term rainfall and evaporation patterns are of interest. In considering the 1975–76 drought these patterns have been typified by the rainfall in 1 month and in 5 and 16 consecutive month periods. The rainfall in any particular month has an immediate effect on the surface run-off and, as will be shown later, the lack of significant rainfall over large areas of the country in June, July and the greater part of August was largely responsible for the very severe conditions in those catchments with a relatively rapid and short-lived baseflow response. The periods of 5 and 16 months are important because of the cumulative effect that occurs either over a single dry summer or over a dry period that includes two summers with the intervening winter. These periods differ significantly from the 8 and 18 months often used in water resources design and were chosen because the rain that fell in late August, September and October made them more appropriate than the longer periods.

The effect of evaporation in relating rainfall to run-off is to reduce the total rainfall to residual rainfall. Part of this evaporation may occur during or immediately after a rainfall event but the majority occurs as evaporation from the upper layers of the soil. The extent of evaporation is limited by the availability of moisture within the upper layer. The Penman method of calculating the evaporation loss is generally used. There is a belief that evaporation losses during the summer are very similar in both wet and dry years because once the available water has been used by the plants further loss occurs at a reduced rate. The relation between the return period of summer rainfall and the return period of the particular low flows which occur in that year is imprecise. Although a few millimetres of additional rainfall can make the difference betewen the one-in-twenty and the one-in-two-hundred-year rainfall event, the additional rainfall will, in a dry year, simply contribute to the evaporation, adding little or nothing to the total stream flow.

Catchment characteristics

The effect of catchment characteristics is fundamental in the temporal distribution of the residual rainfall to stream flow. The major factors are soil type, land use and geology.

In relatively impermeable areas consisting of igneous rocks or stiff clays, as in parts of northern and southwestern England and Wales, the major component of run-off is overland and inter-flow. As a result, river flows in these areas drop rapidly in dry summers and flows in the rivers Elan, Usk and Hodder were very low at the beginning of August 1976 after 3–5 months of low rainfall. In areas where permeable soils overlie the Chalk or sandstone rocks, a much greater percentage of rainfall infiltrates into the upper soil horizons and a proportion reaches the water table to emerge later as base flow. In these catchments, such as the Thames, the Itchen and the Severn, the low flows in 1976 were the cumulative result of a much longer period of rainfall below average.

One of the important factors in determining the relation between rainfall, evaporation, surface run-off, infiltration and percolation with the catchment characteristics of soil type and land use is the soil moisture deficit. This index, regularly calculated by the Meteorological Office, gives an indication of the amount of water required to bring the soil back to field capacity (the ideas used, and their sources, are given by Grindley (1967)). It has an upper limit which is a function of the crop and land use pattern and is related to the root constant for the crop. For example, evaporation from grassland will take place at the potential rate until approximately 80 mm of water have been used. At this point the actual evaporation starts to fall below the potential rate and although the soil moisture deficit continues to increase it does so at a rapidly decreasing rate.

It is sometimes incorrectly assumed that neither surface run-off nor groundwater recharge will take place until the local soil moisture deficit has been reduced to zero. In fact, run-off will occur when the rate of rainfall exceeds the infiltration rate and there is evidence that recharge may commence before the soil moisture deficit has fallen to zero. However, values of soil moisture deficit are frequently used as an indication of catchment state.

While soil type and land use strongly influence the short-term response to residual rainfall, the effect of catchment geology has a very marked effect on base flows. Analysis of flow hydrographs may permit the derivation of a base flow Index and this approach is being followed by the Institute of Hydrology in their low flow studies. An alternative method is the use of a geology Index as developed by the Central Water Planning Unit. During long periods of low flows it is the base flows that predominate and these are related to aquifer storage and response time. Since these properties are often not known, the geology Index may give a practical means of linking the geology with the base flow.

LOW FLOWS 1975–76

The low flows associated with the dry summer of 1976 and the preceding 12 months will be remembered for many years and will undoubtedly be used in the design of water resource schemes. While in terms of rainfall this period produced the driest 16 month period since records began; for river flows, the drought had a wide range of return periods which were often markedly different, even at the same gauging station, for different durations. Here we consider a small sample of the very large number of low flow records that have been analysed since the drought. The results are presented for both flow and rainfall data for catchments of the river Derwent at Yorkshire Bridge, station 28/1; river Great Ouse at Bedford, 33/3; river Thames at Teddington, 39/1; river Itchen at Allbrook, 42/2; river Severn at Bewdley, 54/1; river Elan at Caban Coch reservoir, 55/6; river Usk at Chain Bridge, 56/1; and the river Hodder at Stocks reservoir, 71/2. The locations of these sites, shown on figure 2, were chosen to represent three important aspects of low flows, namely river abstraction points, reservoir inflows, and those sites that have long been used for reference purposes. Further details of each of the catchments may be obtained from the *Surface Water Year Book*. In the text that follows, the catchments are referred to by river and not by the name of the gauging station.

Frequency analysis: choice of distribution

When discussing the return period of a particular event or its probability of occurrence it is necessary to stipulate a frequency distribution, and the choice of distribution is of some importance. Some preference might be given to the use of an automatic fitting procedure which, having fitted the data to the distribution, calculates the magnitude of the event for a particular return interval or, conversely, the return interval of a particular event.

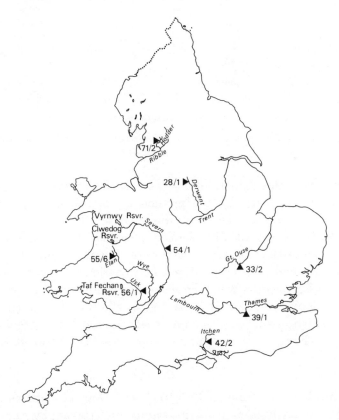

FIGURE 2. Location of rivers and gauging stations.

A uniform approach, similar to that adopted by the Institute of Hydrology and reported by Beran & Gustard (1977), of choosing a single distribution and plotting position, would be ideal. Before considering the choice of distribution it is important to decide what set of random variables should be employed. Any one of a number of possibilities was available. The sets used to give the results quoted in this paper consisted of a single event per annum for the shorter flow periods and sets of non-overlapping records for the longer periods. A random starting date procedure was used and this has the effect, for an event of a given magnitude, of reducing the estimated return period by comparison with stipulating a fixed starting date.

In estimating the parameters of a distribution for a set of random observed variables, a presumption as to the form of the distribution must be made. The distribution having been specified, the parameters may be subjectively determined by graphical techniques.

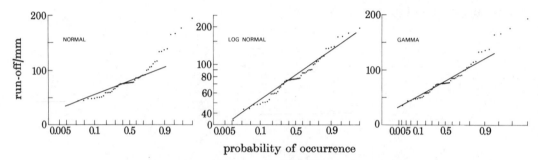

FIGURE 3. Comparison of frequency distributions for 5 month total flow of the river Severn.

In this study, three distributions were tried: normal, log normal and two parameter gamma fitted by the method of moments. (Technical details, too complex for summary, can be supplied on request.) Tests for choice were made on sets of records, for 1 month, for the Ouse, Thames, Itchen, Severn and Usk, and on sets, for 5 and 16 months, for the Severn. Figure 3 shows, for the appropriate generalized Weibull plotting position, the variation that occurs within the three distributions for the Severn for the set of five consecutive month records.

On the basis of this study the log normal distribution was chosen and the Weibull plotting position used. The estimates of return period were obtained from a plot of the data. The line fitting procedure allowed subjective weighting at the lower end.

Rainfall

The Central Water Planning Unit Technical Note 17 contains the results of a comprehensive analysis of rainfall records undertaken by the Meteorological Office. The importance of rainfall on low flows and the choice of 5 and 16 months have been referred to earlier. Figure 4 was derived by the Meteorological Office from the 5 month rainfall map showing percentage of mean from April to August 1976. The return periods, based on a random starting date analysis, were obtained from a detailed analysis of the statistical properties of rainfall records in various parts of England and Wales. Details of given start frequency studies are reported in the Meteorological Office Scientific paper no. 37.

The map shows the wide variation in return period over very small distances, as, for example, the figures of once in more than 200 years in Nottinghamshire and once in less than five years in Northamptonshire. This reinforces the earlier

statement that relatively small rainfalls can affect the return periods very substantially; the difference in this case arose from local storms in Northamptonshire,
which occurred in both July and August 1976. However, the map also explains why
there were crucial shortages in the inflow to the reservoirs in north Wales where
run-off is highly correlated with the 5 month rainfall. It also indicates the extensive
areas of rainfall deficiency along the south and southwestern coasts of England.

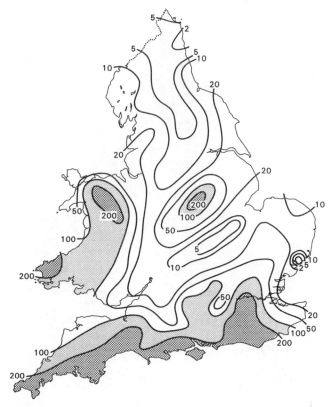

FIGURE 4. Frequency of occurrence of 5 month rainfall in England and Wales. April to
August 1976, based on a random starting date analysis. Information supplied by the
Meteorological Office.

Figure 5 shows rainfall as a percentage of average over England and Wales for
the 16 months from May 1975 to August 1976. It is the combination of the effects
of the 5 and 16 month periods that were of particular importance in the chalk
catchments of Southern England where areas that had rainfall of only 50–60 %
of average over the longer period had for the last 5 months of that period an event
with a return interval of more than 100 years and in some areas in excess of
200 years.

The rainfall statistics for the eight catchments are given in table 1. The mean
catchment rainfall for both the Thames and the Itchen is greater than the monthly

average for only 1 month between April 1975 and August 1976, whereas there are six such events on the river Hodder. Significant rain fell in many catchments in September 1975 and May 1976 but apart from those two months there is little discernible pattern between the rainfall events. Rainfall in January 1976 ranged from 21 % of the monthly average on the Itchen to 151 % on the Derwent and in April 1976 from 21 % on the Usk to 48 % on the Hodder.

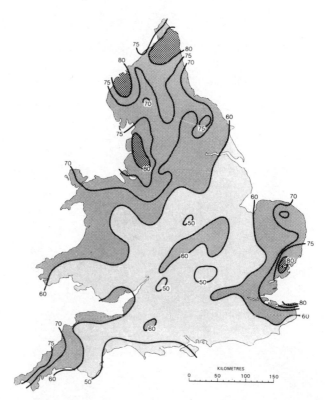

FIGURE 5. Rainfall as a percentage of the 16 month long-term average: May 1975 to August 1976. Information supplied by the Meteorological Office.

The results of a more detailed study of the rainfall and the soil moisture deficits for the Thames and the Usk are given in table 2. The figures for the Usk show that the soil moisture deficit values for 1975 reached a maximum of 108 mm in mid-August and then decreased to zero by the beginning of January 1976. They began to increase again in March 1976, reaching a maximum of 131 mm just before the rains fell at the end of August. The estimated soil moisture deficit values in the Usk catchment were greater in both 1975 and 1976 than any values in the previous 35 years. This feature of 1975 and 1976 giving the highest values during the period of record was common to much of the country. It is worth remembering that soil moisture deficits are estimates and not actual field measurements.

TABLE 1. MONTHLY RAINFALL FOR SELECTED CATCHMENT AREAS

1975

river and gauge	Apr.	May	June	July	Aug.	Sept.	Oct.	Nov.	Dec.
Derwent at Yorkshire Bridge									
mm	116	77	26	107	66	77	56	90	102
% average	120	84	30	98	56	69	39	59	74
Great Ouse at Bedford									
mm	61	48	18	43	21	79	17	38	28
% average	120	91	42	67	36	141	28	58	50
Thames at Teddington									
mm	47	47	12	39	27	108	19	55	30
% average	87	85	27	57	43	177	26	71	43
Itchen at Allbrook									
mm	51	47	10	59	45	146	30	75	37
% average	88	89	21	83	65	212	35	77	41
Severn at Bewdley									
mm	68	42	20	67	53	70	35	64	59
% average	108	59	34	80	63	95	36	66	66
Elan at Caban Coch									
mm	128	41	23	125	70	183	80	175	132
% average	109	38	21	88	47	122	40	86	64
Usk at Chain Bridge									
mm	70	34	17	119	78	161	64	89	85
% average	79	40	23	120	72	155	44	59	57
Hodder at Stocks Reservoir									
mm	104	25	29	181	114	236	98	145	90
% average	108	27	29	135	73	153	53	88	56

1976

river and gauge	Jan.	Feb.	Mar.	Apr.	May	June	July	Aug.	Sept.
Derwent at Yorkshire Bridge									
mm	246	67	80	39	139	16	29	17	157
% average	159	55	90	40	151	19	27	15	140
Great Ouse at Bedford									
mm	25	18	22	14	37	19	26	28	92
% average	43	42	54	27	70	44	41	48	164
Thames at Teddington									
mm	21	27	22	13	32	21	27	26	116
% average	30	52	47	24	58	47	40	41	190
Itchen at Allbrook									
mm	19	39	22	13	29	17	39	13	151
% average	21	61	39	22	55	35	55	19	219
Severn at Bewdley									
mm	72	55	62	17	71	17	33	14	209
% average	73	81	102	27	100	29	39	17	282
Elan at Caban Coch									
mm	176	109	98	32	108	19	50	19	203
% average	81	68	84	27	101	18	35	13	135
Usk at Chain Bridge									
mm	80	74	76	19	80	21	39	53	241
% average	49	66	81	21	93	28	39	49	232
Hodder at Stocks Reservoir									
mm	222	86	112	46	152	34	71	36	147
% average	117	67	119	48	167	34	53	23	95

Run-off

The magnitude of low flows can be presented in several ways, each of which is used to illustrate a different aspect. For most engineers and scientists in the water industry the hydrograph of river flow gives an immediate feel for the position. Figure 6 shows the flow hydrograph for each of the selected catchments for the period from 1 April 1975 to 30 September 1976 inclusive.

TABLE 2. CUMULATIVE RAINFALL AND ESTIMATED SOIL MOISTURE DEFICIT
(millimetres) FOR TWO CATCHMENTS IN 1975–76

catchment	Thames to Teddington		Usk to Chain Bridge	
date	cumulative rainfall	soil moisture deficit	cumulative rainfall	soil moisture deficit
1 April 1975	0	0	0	0
May	47	6	70	4
June	94	39	104	16
July	106	92	121	95
August	145	123	240	93
September	172	133	318	93
October	280	104	479	58
November	299	78	543	29
December	354	36	632	7
January 1976	384	31	717	2
February	405	24	797	0
March	432	21	871	1
April	454	28	947	4
May	467	61	966	36
June	499	98	1046	54
July	520	130	1067	82
August	547	136	1106	114
September	573	143	1159	120
October	689	69	1400	48

The continuous monthly flow hydrograph for 1975–76 is compared with the discontinuous values of mean flow and minimum previously recorded values. It must be emphasized that neither the mean nor the minimum values ever occur, as a continuous sequence. This figure illustrates once again the very marked difference between the response of river flow to rainfall both with time in a given catchment and between catchments with different characteristics. The February 1976 rainfall of 39 mm in the Itchen produced a response, whereas a similar rainfall in July 1976, when the evaporation and soil moisture deficits were large, did not. The immediate response of the river Elan to the September 1976 rainfall of 183 mm was in marked contrast to the more subdued response of the river Thames to 108 mm in the same month. This was in part due to the difference between the rainfall received and the prevailing soil moisture deficits. Nevertheless it also indicates a significant difference in catchment response.

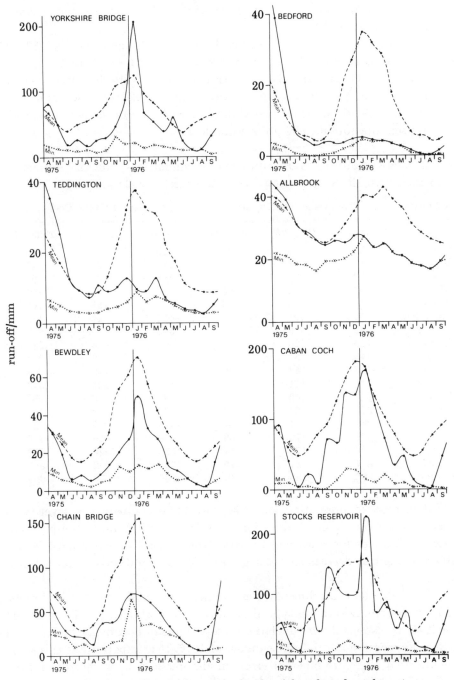

FIGURE 6. Flow hydrographs for the eight selected catchments
April 1975 to September 1976.

A second method for computing flow values is to tabulate the cumulative flows and the cumulative monthly mean values. This information is presented in table 3 for the rivers Thames and Elan.

Table 3 shows the cumulative flows for the 1975–76 drought and the 1933–34 drought. If April is taken as the starting month, the 1933–34 drought was more severe for both the Thames and the Elan. In both catchments the lowest one and two consecutive month values occurred in 1976. The cumulative values of flow for the Thames in 1975–76 can be compared directly with the concurrent cumulative rainfall and soil moisture deficits given in table 2.

TABLE 3. MEAN CUMULATIVE FLOW VALUES (millimetres) FOR THE RIVERS THAMES AND ELAN COMPARED WITH FLOWS IN 1933–34 AND 1975–76

catchment	Thames at Teddington			Elan at Caban Coch		
month	mean	1975–76	1933–34	mean	1975–76	1933–34
April	23	36	23	80	92	15
May	40	61	41	139	133	40
June	52	73	50	186	137	94
July	62	83	58	242	159	157
August	70	90	63	321	168	166
September	79	101	69	412	240	172
October	92	109	76	540	307	289
November	115	120	83	701	444	346
December	146	132	89	883	578	374
January	183	142	99	1055	746	554
February	216	151	106	1181	863	573
March	247	159	118	1284	935	691
April	270	165	128	1364	969	763
May	287	171	134	1423	1016	825
June	299	175	138	1470	1026	840
July	309	178	141	1526	1030	852
August	317	181	145	1605	1032	967
September	326	186	149	1696	1079	1000

A third method of presenting low flow data is to compare the severity of recorded events over different durations. Table 4 gives a ranked list of low flows for the Thames for a period of record from 1883. The eight most severe events are ranked in decreasing order of severity for durations between 1 and 18 months.

Data from all eight catchments were ranked to obtain probability plots. Figure 7 for the river Severn is a typical example. This particular graph is included because it shows the maximum deviation from the line of best fit for the 1, 2 and 3 month flows measured during the summer of 1976. It is important at this stage to recognize that there are inherent errors in all stream gauging records and the value of 4 m³/s (2.5 mm of run-off), which is the average naturalized August 1976 flow for the river Severn at Bewdley, is subject to these errors. It would not be appropriate to discuss errors in any detail here but such a discussion would

TABLE 4. SEVERITY OF HISTORIC LOW FLOW SEQUENCES,†
RIVER THAMES AT TEDDINGTON (1883–1976)

duration	rank							
month	1	2	3	4	5	6	7	8
1	1976	1921	1898	1944	1899	1949	1934	1906
2	1976	1921	1944	1988	1949	1934	1899	1906
3	1921	1976	1944	1934	1949	1898	1899	1906
4	1921	1944	1934	1976	1899	1949	1896	1929
5	1934	1921	1944	1976	1899	1898	1929	1901
6	1921	1934	1944	1976	1899	1901	1793	1929
8	1921	1934	1944	1976	1899	1901	1933–4	1943
9	1921	1934	1944	1976	1933–4	1943–4	1898	1899
10	1921–2	1934	1944	1975–6	1902	1898	1890–1	1899
12	1933–4	1943–4	1975–6	1921–2	1901–2	1890–1	1904–5	1897–8
16	1933–4	1943–4	1975–6	1901–2	1890–1	1904–5	1897–8	1921–2
17	1933–4	1943–4	1901–2	1975–6	1890–1	1904–5	1897–8	1921–2
18	1933–4	1943–4	1901–2	1890–1	1975–6	1904–5	1921–2	1897–8

† The low flows are ranked, one event per calendar year, by using a random starting date
analysis and non-overlapping events, based upon measured naturalized flows.

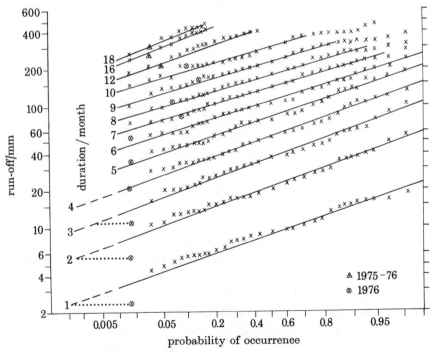

FIGURE 7. Frequency of occurrence of low flow events: river Severn at Bewdley.

include errors in measurement and errors in naturalizing procedure. The latter includes inaccuracies in measured abstractions and returns and errors arising from unauthorized abstraction. For most of the analysis the archived records of the Water Data Unit were used, assuming that they represent the best available information. Where there have been apparent inconsistencies the records have been checked directly with the appropriate water authority.

Once every catchment had been analysed in a similar manner a summary of the information was prepared and this is presented in table 5. The figures in table 5 give an estimate of the reciprocal frequency of occurrence of low flows (as years per event) in each of the catchments for the drought of 1975–76.

THE EFFECT OF THE DROUGHT ON RIVER SYSTEMS

In order to appreciate the impact of low flows on river systems it is necessary to consider the range of uses to which rivers are put and the effect that droughts of increasing severity will have. It is also important to recognize that for some uses it is the short-term low flows that are critical whereas for others it is the longer periods of shortages that are of concern.

TABLE 5. RETURN PERIOD (years) OF LOW FLOW EVENTS,† 1975–76

years of record	river gauge	duration/month										
		1	2	3	4	5	6	8	9	10	16	18
63	Yorkshire Bridge	25	40	25	15	9	10	10	7	8	25	15
44	Bedford	50	35	20	20	20	20	20	20	25	20	20
94	Teddington	90	70	50	35	30	30	30	35	35	30	20
18	Allbrook‡	40	40	50	50	30	70	50	50	35	20	15
56	Bewdley‡	200+	200+	200+	100	60	35	15	7	7	45	30
69	Caban Coch	100	200+	200+	45	70	70	30	8	9	40	40
20	Chain Bridge‡	50	200	100	100	60	30	20	15	15	30	25
50	Stocks Reservoir	10	20	100	10	7	9	7	4	4	5	9

† Based upon measured naturalized flows, random starting date non-overlapping events.
‡ See also table 7 with alternative values based upon an extended record.

Table 5 indicates the very wide range of return period of occurrence of the low flows that were experienced during the years 1975 and 1976. There are notable variations between catchments and between the return intervals of different periods for the same catchment. For example, the driest 1 month during 1976 has a return interval of ten years for the river Hodder at Stocks reservoir while for the river Severn at Bewdley it is something in excess of 200 years. The return period of the 2 and 4 month sequences at Stocks are quite moderate but the three month period has a return interval of about 100 years. This variation is of course largely explained by the rainfall pattern in 1976 shown in table 1 for Stocks reservoir.

Although for the Thames at Teddington the 1976 drought was the most severe on record for 1 and 2 month sequences, table 4 shows that it ranked second for a 3 month sequence and only fourth for sequences of 4–10 months.

This pattern is typical. For the river Elan the 1975–76 flows were rank one for periods of 1, 2, 3, 5 and 6 months; rank two for periods of 4, 8, 16 and 18 months and lower ranks for the other periods analysed. On the river Hodder 1976 was the rank one event only for the 3 month period, and on the river Derwent it was never the rank one event and was rank two only for periods of 1, 2 and 3 months.

It was the rivers with shorter flow records where the 1975–76 event was consistently the worst recorded. Thus for the river Itchen it was rank one for all periods of 1–18 months and for the river Usk rank one for all periods except that of 10 months duration.

This variation makes it difficult to reply to the question 'How severe was the drought of 1975–76?' in a way which would adequately cover the complex situation. Nevertheless it is possible to survey the effect of the low flows on particular river systems in respect of particular uses.

The most important use of many rivers, at least during periods of low flows, is for water supply. This may take place either directly from reservoirs, which are affected by the reduction in inflow, or by river abstraction from regulated or non-regulated rivers. In both direct supply and abstraction from regulated rivers it is the 5 to 18 month flow patterns that are important. For the abstraction from non-regulated rivers either to supply or to pumped storage reservoirs it is the current rate of flow that is critical and longer periods are important primarily because of the progressive measures that have to be taken to restrict demand.

The impact of the drought on the river system can be known with certainty only in the upper reaches of the catchment. Downstream flows reflect a large number of effects and are the integrated result of reduced natural run-off, increased abstraction for agricultural use, reduced draw-off for supply, reduced return flows from wastewater treatment works, leakage into riparian areas and evaporation losses. Finally, there were the remedial measures taken by some water authorities to supplement river flows and thus minimize the effect of the drought on the rivers within their area.

Reservoirs

The reservoirs listed in table 6 are in two categories. Clywedog is a regulating reservoir used to release water down the river Severn for later abstraction, both upstream and downstream of Bewdley, and to maintain a minimum flow in the river at Bewdley. The other five reservoirs are used for direct supply to urban areas and at the time of their construction each represented a single source of water. To some extent all of them have now become part of a large water resource system so that they no longer represent the sole source of supply to their original demand area. They were all subject to severe restriction in their inflows both in 1975 and 1976. However, by the use of alternative sources, or by restriction in demand, or by a reduction in the statutory compensation releases, or by a combination of these measures, there was some limitation in the amount of water that was abstracted. It is therefore very difficult to compare the severity of the 1975–76 drought directly with reservoir contents. This is particularly true of the Taf Fechan reservoirs where, had it not been for an increasingly rigorous set of restrictions, the reservoir levels would have fallen disastrously below the 22 % level obtaining at the end of August.

TABLE 6. RESERVOIR CONTENTS FOR THE PERIOD
APRIL 1975 – SEPTEMBER 1976

(Values given are the volume in store on the first day of the month
as a percentage of maximum capacity.)

reservoir	Apr.	May	June	July	Aug.	Sept.	Oct.	Nov.	Dec.
					1975				
Clywedog	93	97	96	86	71	53	45	53	64
Vyrnwy	93	95	88	75	69	60	52	56	60
Elan Valley	94	96	92	77	68	54	48	52	55
Derwent Valley	100	100	95	78	65	48	36	30	35
Stocks	74	75	68	54	62	45	60	60	60
Taf Fechan	96	93	80	61	58	47	50	47	54

	Jan.	Feb.	Mar.	Apr.	May	June	July	Aug.	Sept.	Oct.
					1976					
Clywedog	78	89	93	96	97	95	82	50	27	29
Vyrnwy	75	86	91	88	83	75	63	50	37	52
Elan Valley	78	88	97	93	88	82	68	53	37	33
Derwent Valley	58	93	96	93	93	93	84	72	55	52
Stocks	60	96	88	83	73	76	58	44	30	29
Taf Fechan	55	61	63	61	54	51	42	29	22	35

The low reservoir levels in August 1976 caused considerable concern, because they were then generally lower than previous levels in August, either for 1975 or for earlier dry years. Nor was there any reason to suppose that the drought might not continue into September and October. Thus Vyrnwy was at 60 % of capacity on the first of September 1975 and at 37 % capacity on the first of September 1976. The figures for the Elan Valley are 54 and 37 % respectively and for Taf Fechan 47 and 22 % respectively. Of the reservoirs listed only those in the Derwent Valley were not significantly worse in 1976. A study of the records shows that inflows to the Derwent reservoirs for both 9 and 10 months duration were smaller in 1975 than they were in 1976. This extreme variability of the flows in 1975–76 was highlighted earlier in table 5.

Rivers

The effect of the drought on rivers of England and Wales was such that for many of the records examined the lowest flows occurred in August 1976. Widespread rainfall at the end of the month masks just how severe the low flows were, because the average values for August do not disclose the worst situation, which occurred during the middle of the month.

There are two parameters of importance in assessing the effect of low flows on rivers. The first is the low flow itself and the second, equally important, is the quality of the water.

At all river abstraction points there is a prescribed flow below which abstractions are not normally permitted. The intention of setting the prescribed flow is to safeguard the quality of the river downstream and protect the rights of downstream riparian owners. There were many instances last summer when Orders had to be sought to reduce the level of the prescribed flow. It is remarkable that the quality of water downstream was, in the vast majority of rivers, unaffected by this decision. Whether this is due to too conservative an estimate of the prescribed flow or to the compensating effects of the very high level of sunshine and photosynthesis in 1976 is uncertain. It is unlikely, however, that the prescribed flows could have been reduced to the same levels in October and November without considerable risk of a deterioration in river quality.

During 1976 there was concern that much of the water released from regulation reservoirs was being lost to river gravels and bankside storage. If this were true over a prolonged period of release then the whole concept of regulated rivers would be open to question because they were designed particularly to guard against the effects of such severe droughts. To lose a significant proportion of releases when severe droughts occur would negate their construction. It now appears that on two highly regulated rivers, the Severn and the Dee, these losses over the summer were not significant.

However, on some rivers losses did occur to riverside gravels and into the land adjacent to the river bank. On the Thames there were losses in a 36 km stretch between the Eynsham and Days gauging stations where in early July 1976 the loss was estimated at about 65 Ml/d. As the river levels fell during August the magnitude of this loss also declined.

In the Anglian Water Authority area the ponded river Ely Ouse above Denver received an average inflow of some 150 Ml/d during July and August 1976, all of which was lost by evaporation, or withdrawal into the fenland via sluices or by subsurface flow. Thus during those months there was no flow from this river into the estuary.

Remedial measures

Water authorities faced with a situation when supply is threatened can either reduce compensation flows or develop alternative sources. The National Water Council publication *The 1975–76 drought* and the drought reports of the ten water authorities summarize the steps which were taken over the country as a whole.

There were some authorities who took steps designed not only to supplement supplies but also to maintain the low flows in the river system at an acceptable level for water supply purposes and to maintain river water quality. Two schemes are worthy of mention.

The development by the Thames Conservancy and subsequently by the Thames Water Authority of the scheme to supplement flows in the Lambourn and adjacent

Pang streams in the Berkshire Downs has evoked great interest among water and river engineers. In summarizing the effect of the first operational use of the well field in the late summer of 1976, B. J. Hardcastle (1977, personal communication) notes that the flows in both streams were restored to their normal perennial level and that successful augmentation in excess of 72×10^3 Ml (72 Gl) was carried out over a period of approximately 3 months until the rapid recovery of groundwater levels, which occurred in mid-November.

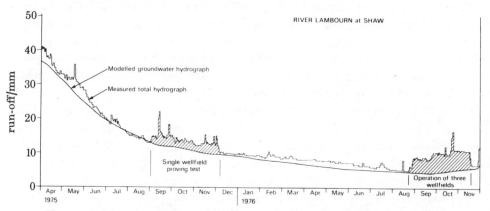

FIGURE 8. River flow augmentation by groundwater abstraction: Thames basin. Prepared by the Thames Conservancy Division, Thames Water.

The effect of pumping and the clear indication of net gain during the pumping period is shown in figure 8. Losses at the distant boundaries and when pumping ceased are still being investigated.

The second scheme, by the Anglian Water Authority, was to reverse the flow along the length of the river Great Ouse between Offord and Earith by the installation of pumps at the seven locks in this reach of the river. The proposal to pump 65 Ml/d would, with the flow coming downstream at Offord, permit a minimum abstraction of 130 Ml/d to be maintained. This proposal relied on the concept that the maintenance of a minimum prescribed flow is not necessarily directionally important. Thus the pumping upstream in a ponded river of 65 Ml/d from an adjacent catchment is equivalent to a minimum downstream flow of 65 Ml/d and gives a net yield upstream of 130 Ml/d. In the event, although the engineering work was complete by October the need for the scheme had passed.

A similar scheme for pumping back over four weirs was actually operated by the Thames Water Authority on a much smaller scale at a rate between 9 and 13 Ml/d to a temporary intake immediately below Eynsham weir.

MATHEMATICAL MODELS FOR FLOW PREDICTION
AND FREQUENCY ANALYSIS

One of the most difficult management problems during the course of a drought is the need for decisions that are influenced by assumptions of future river flow. This was of particular concern in 1976 when the position was already critical in some areas by the middle of August and the possibility of a further 3 months of dry weather could not be discounted. Indeed, a study by the Meteorological Office shows that it would have been extremely unwise to discount the possibility of the 1976–77 winter having rainfall less than average. However, some decisions were based on assumptions of rainfall or run-off that were extreme. For example, while the probability of having 6 months of winter rainfall of only 50 % of the long average in Hampshire is of the order of once in 100 years, in Cumberland the probability of a similar event is less than once in 500 years. The probability of having 50 % of the long average rainfall for 12 consecutive months is so rare that no confidence can be placed on any estimate of the return period.

What is necessary, therefore, is to present the information in terms that show clearly the consequences of particular courses of action given clearly stated probabilities of future rainfall or river flows. This will enable logical decisions to be taken.

This may be attempted in one of three ways. The use of data generation techniques, the use of rainfall statistics where these are easier to obtain than adequate river flow data, or the use of flow records where they are of sufficient length to permit realistic statistical analysis.

Of these methods the use of synthetic data generation has not yet been developed to the point where it is acceptable in the framework of operational management. The statistical use of flow data suffers because the prediction of future flow on a given start frequency analysis does not make any allowance for the current catchment state. The use of rainfall statistics, if it is possible to derive a satisfactory rainfall run-off model, gives the most promising method and warrants further research and development.

Synthetic data generation

K. H. Tattersall, in a presentation to the National Water Council seminar on the 1975–76 drought, stated that in order to make progress in river management during droughts one must study droughts as occurrences. The use of synthetic data, he asserted, is merely to add confusion to an already complex subject. The first statement cannot be disputed; the second is open to argument.

One of the possibilities that synthetic data give is to study sequences of low flow events that are not disclosed in the historic record. This permits a study of droughts and allows an estimate to be made of the probability of dry winters with less than average run-off following exceptionally dry summers.

The record at Bewdley was extended to give eight 50-year sequences of flow.

A study of these synthetic sequences, using a random starting date, gives rank-one 5 month flows of 42.8, 48.7, 24.3, 44.0, 41.8, 33.8, 41.6 and 43.6 mm compared with the observed Bewdley value in 1976 of 36.3 mm. Of the eight sequences, more than half were followed by winters drier than average.

Mathematical models based on rainfall–run-off relations

During the drought of 1976 several water authorities used catchment models to assess the possible situation during the winter of 1976–77. They were requested to estimate the water situation if the monthly rainfall continued at 100, 75 and 50 % of the long-term average for a further 12 months (National Water Council 1976, p. 8). This exercise is relatively easy to carry out provided that suitable catchment models exist, but it has two shortcomings. First, rainfall at 50 % of average is quite probable for 1 or 2 months in succession, but highly unlikely for prolonged periods such as a year. The probability of occurrence changes as the period increases if the fraction is fixed. The second objection is that 75 or 50 % of average rainfall does not have the same frequency of occurrence in different parts of the country. A better method of forward planning is to assume given values of rainfall probability and estimate the resultant river flows and reservoir levels.

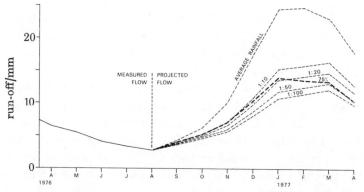

FIGURE 9. Flow projection of the river Thames at Teddington.

In the autumn of 1976 both conceptual and regression models were used for flow projection to assess the probable water situation during the ensuing winter months. For many flow projection purposes, models easy to use are adequate. Existing procedures for flow projection in a drought are not highly refined in most catchments with significant water resources. However, catchment models relating river flows to weather are available for over 70 catchments in England and Wales. Many of these are based upon regression methods such as those developed at the Central Water Planning Unit.

Figure 9 illustrates a flow projection for the river Thames at Teddington for specified rainfall probabilities compared with projections based upon 75 % of average rainfall persisting month after month.

Care should be taken in this exercise to use the correct rainfall probability tables. For flow projection the rainfall probability analyses should be based upon a given starting date. Suitable probability tables were circulated to the Water Authorities for hydrometric areas and individual catchments in the late summer of 1976. These were prepared by the Meteorological Office and circulated by the Central Water Planning Unit; an example for the Thames basin is shown in table 7.

A second use of the equations is to extend flow records to permit estimates of the frequency of occurrence of low flow events based on additional records. A project at the Central Water Planning Unit included the extension of flow records based upon catchment models and historic weather records. The frequency of occurrence of selected droughts over the past 100 years is shown for durations of

TABLE 7. SEVERITY OF SPECIFIED DRY PERIODS FOR THE
THAMES BASIN, STARTING IN A GIVEN MONTH

(Figures expressed as a percentage of average rainfall in 1911–70.)

reciprocal frequency of occurrence (1 in x years)	duration of dry period/month						
	1	2	3	4	6	9	12
5	57	69	74	78	82	85	87
10	38	55	63	67	73	78	81
20	25	44	53	59	66	72	75
50	13	32	43	50	58	65	70
100	8	25	37	44	53	61	66
200	5	19	31	39	49	57	62

TABLE 8. RETURN PERIOD (years) OF HISTORIC LOW FLOW EVENTS AT THREE
STATIONS BASED UPON AN EXTENDED FLOW RECORD†

years of record	river and gauge	year	duration/month										
			1	2	3	4	5	6	8	9	10	16	18
96	Itchen at	1921–2	35	35	50	50	50	80	90	80	70	7	8
(1881–	Allbrook	1943–4	10	15	15	15	12	15	15	15	15	40	40
1976)		1975–6	—	—	—	—	—	—	—	—	—	30	15
		1976	100	50	60	60	50	40	35	35	35	—	—
94	Severn at	1920–1	15	15	10	10	15	35	40	50	60	15	10
(1883–	Bewdley	1933–4	35	50	15	15	15	35	100	200	100	100	120
1976)		1975	20	12	20	25	25	20	15	20	20	—	—
		1975–6	—	—	—	—	—	—	—	—	—	70	50
		1976	200+	200+	200+	200	100	50	10	8	5	—	—
97	Usk at	1920–1	20	15	12	8	15	30	50	50	80	6	5
(1880–	Chain	1933–4	7	9	6	5	8	8	7	15	8	30	45
1976)	Bridge	1975	7	7	7	9	5	5	8	10	—	—	—
		1975–6	—	—	—	—	—	—	—	—	25	120	100
		1976	100	150	100	45	80	25	15	15	—	—	—

† Based upon an extended flow record derived from historic weather data and a catchment model, random starting date analysis, one event per calendar year and non-overlapping events.

1–18 months in table 8 for three such extended records. The 1921 drought was exceptionally severe over 8 month durations in southern and eastern England, the Midlands and Wales, and was estimated to be appreciably more severe for this duration than the 1975–76 drought for the three catchments analysed in table 8.

One reason for the 1921 drought's being more severe than 1976 for the 8 month duration – critical for most small reservoirs – is that the rainfall deficiency in 1921 persisted into September and October. Two other points of interest arise from table 8. For periods in excess of 7 months, 1933–34 was more severe than 1975–76 in the Severn catchment. The other point is the significantly different return periods for the Usk for 16 and 18 months duration when comparing values in tables 5 and 8. This emphasizes the difficulty of obtaining reliable estimates of return period for long rare events from relatively short records.

The statistical analysis of historic run-off data

Where the catchment in question is one with a long flow record and has a quick catchment response the use of run-off statistics provides a third method of flow projection. The example quoted is for the Derwent reservoirs of the Severn Trent Water Authority and was chosen because it fulfils the criterion of a rapid catchment response and because it had a very significant draw down in 1975. In the event it was, for 1976, the least affected of the reservoirs listed in table 6.

TABLE 9. ESTIMATED CUMULATIVE MONTHLY INFLOWS (gigalitres per month)
TO THE DERWENT VALLEY SYSTEM OF RESERVOIRS

starting month and probabilities of occurrence

	July			August			September			actual inflows 1976
month	1%	2%	4%	1%	2%	4%	1%	2%	4%	
July	0.6	0.9	1.3	—	—	—	—	—	—	0.94
Aug.	2.1	2.7	3.7	0.5	0.8	1.2	—	—	—	0.84
Sept.	4.1	5.3	6.9	2.1	2.7	3.8	0.4	0.6	1.0	40.00
Oct.	9.6	11.4	14.2	6.7	8.5	10.6	4.0	5.0	6.4	
Nov.	21.3	24.5	28.1	17.5	20.3	23.4	13.2	15.4	18.1	
Dec	33.9	38.0	42.5	29.6	33.2	37.8	25.2	28.4	32.5	
Jan.	52.8	57.3	62.8	48.6	53.1	57.7	42.9	47.0	51.5	
Feb.	64.4	69.4	75.7	59.5	65.0	70.4	53.4	58.3	63.8	
Mar.	75.5	81.4	87.8	70.7	76.2	82.5	64.1	69.5	75.4	
Apr.	83.3	89.6	96.9	78.5	84.4	91.1	72.0	77.2	84.0	

A fixed starting date analysis is carried out to estimate the cumulative inflows over a period of months for a range of probabilities. Table 9 gives for starting dates of 1 July, 1 August and 1 September the inflows with 1, 2 and 4% probability which may be expected over the following winter to the end of April.

If the analysis is used to project reservoir storages following the known reservoir contents on the first of August, then a trace may be obtained for each of a range of demand levels stipulating a given probability of inflow. Figure 10 shows that the results for two probabilities of inflow and for demands that range from 200 Ml/d plus a compensation release of 76 Ml/d to a demand of 160 Ml/d plus a compensation release of 38 Ml/d.

For none of the demand patterns investigated would the reservoir storage have fallen below the desirable minimum level in November unless the drought were more severe than the 1 % event. An estimate of inflow probability can be made

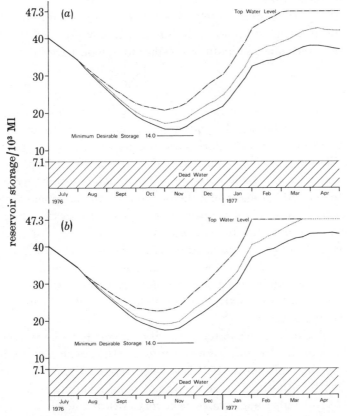

FIGURE 10. Projection of reservoir storage for 1 % (*a*) and 2 % (*b*) inflows and a range of demands: Derwent reservoirs. Daily demands: ———, 200 + 76 Ml; ·····, 182 + 76 Ml; —·—, 182 + 38 Ml.

from a knowledge of the July inflow and appears to be approximately 2 %. The procedure enables the position to be updated each week so that the consequences of changes in the demand pattern can be monitored, as can revised estimates of the severity of the drought. Thus on 1 September the observed August inflow of 840 Ml is in accord with the estimate of a 2 % probability.

A comparison between the return interval of the 1 month event of once in 25 years given in table 5 and once in 50 years deduced from table 9 shows the difference in results obtained when considering a fixed rather than a random starting date for the analysis.

If for operational purposes it were decided that a storage of 90 % of capacity at the end of April was desirable, then on 1 August it would be possible to say that if the drought in the Derwent Valley had a 1 % probability of occurrence, a cut in demand of 200–180 Ml/d would be necessary. A reduction in the compensation releases would, however, have been unnecessary. On the basis of the analysis for a 2 % probability, the full demand could have been sustained all winter during the 2 % year without restriction.

Similar analyses for the more severely affected reservoirs would have given the level of restriction in demand appropriate for each inflow probability to achieve stated objectives in terms of minimum reservoir storage on particular dates.

Conclusion

There is no definitive answer to the question 'how severe was the effect of the 1975–76 drought on river flows?' The question can only be answered for a stated duration on a specified river. For short durations on certain rivers, of which the Severn and the Elan are specific examples, the event was very severe indeed with an average interval in excess of 200 years, that is a probability of occurrence in any year of 0.005. For periods of eight months or more it was in some catchments a notable event with an average return period of 50 years. In parts of England and Wales there have been more severe droughts in the recent past. For example, the drought on the river Hodder was unremarkable for the eight month duration.

The effect of the drought on rivers was certainly less dramatic than pronouncements made last year would have led one to expect. Even for the Severn where the flows in July and August were extremely rare the river suffered no apparent ill effects nor any lasting damage.

Although with hindsight some water authorities might have been overcautious last year the effects of the drought were minimized with considerable skill. Nevertheless if the very dry autumn of 1921 had been repeated in 1976, and no one could have said with authority that it would not be, the supply position in some areas at the end of November might have been very critical indeed.

The development of adequate management models for use during drought periods is of considerable importance.

We acknowledge the help received from many of our colleagues during the preparation of this paper and in particular the Meteorological Office which supplied the rainfall data.

BIBLIOGRAPHY (Hamlin & Wright)

Beran, M. A. & Gustard, A. 1977 A study into the low-flow characteristics of British rivers. *J. Hydrol.* **35**, 147–157.

Central Water Planning Unit 1976 *The 1975–76 drought: a hydrological review.* Tech. Note 17 (35 pages).

Central Water Planning Unit 1976 A geology index for river flow studies. *C.W.P.U. Annual Report 1975–76*, pp. 53–55.

Dawdy, D. R. & O'Donnell, T. 1965 Mathematical Models of Catchment Behaviour. *J. A.S.C.E.* **90**, H 7.4., 123–137.

Grindley, J. 1967 The estimation of soil moisture deficits. *Met. Mag.* **96**, 97–108.

Hamlin, M. J., Fisher, R. G. & Cluckie, I. D. 1975 Multi-site data generation for large water resource systems. *I.A.H.S. Symposium, Bratislava* (26 pages).

Meaden, G. T. 1977 North West Europe's great drought – the worst in Britain since 1252–1253? *J. Met.* **1**, 379–383.

National Water Council 1976 *Water supply prospectus for 1977* (29 pages).

National Water Council 1977 *The 1975–76 drought* (48 pages).

Paris, M. 1884 *Matthaei Parisiensis Monachi Sancti Albani Chronica Majora V. Rolls Series 1872–84.*

Penman, H. L. 1948 Natural evaporation from open water, bare soil and grass. *Proc. R. Soc. Lond.* A **193**, 120–145.

Tabony, R. G. 1977 The variability of long duration rainfall over Great Britain. *Met. Off. Scientific Paper* No. 37.

Thom, A. S. & Oliver, H. R. 1977 On Penman's equation for estimating regional evaporation. *Q. Jl R. met. Soc.* **103**, 345–357.

Water Resources Board 1974 *The surface water year book of Great Britain 1966–70* (160 pages). London: H.M.S.O.

Wright, C. E. 1974 The influence of catchment characteristics upon low flows in S.E. England. *Wat. Ser.* **78**, 227–230.

Discussion

W. L. JACK (*Welsh Water Authority, Cambrian Way, Brecon, U.K.*). I should like to ask Professor Hamlin two points.

First, by using scales other than the usual ones, the return periods derived have different meanings to the return periods derived by, for example the Welsh, North West and Severn/Trent Water Authorities.

Secondly, Professor Hamlin has said that rainfall severities are different from run-off severities. Would he agree that for most water resources work maps of run-off severity would be much more useful than maps of rainfall severity?

M. J. HAMLIN AND C. E. WRIGHT.

(*a*) The probability scale chosen was the one found to be most appropriate to the data which was analysed and for durations of relevance to water supplies. Other scales would give similar return periods for all the rarer events. In our paper we put an upper limit of 1 in 200 years or longer, which should minimize any discrepancies due to the choice of different scales.

(*b*) Maps of run-off severity are an admirable idea but difficult to obtain in practice due to the short length of most flow records. Reliable estimates of the frequency of occurrence of the 1975–76 low flows, especially over the longer durations, are not readily obtained from short records.

B. RYDZ (6, *Kingsdown House, Box, Corsham, Wiltshire, SN14 9AX, U.K.*). I should like to emphasize a point embedded in Professor Hamlin's paper. Any water resource project must be designed to a given reliability or risk, whether specified or implicit. It happens that, in many areas, last year's events came close to the extreme for which British engineers have designed for about the past century. Since one designs with an assumption of foresight but operates without it, a 'design year' is normally one in which we begin to get into trouble. This happened in several areas last year, apart from some which had been unable to keep their resources up to par and, therefore, suffered fairly serious deprivation.

Almost any reliability of supply which the consumer is likely to desire can be provided in this country at a tolerable price, but it will still be limited and, if we are to design rationally, a worse-than-design year will mean the acceptance of deprivation. The most important things we have to learn from a drought are the most acceptable patterns of deprivation and their economic consequences for industry. By visualizing these at the design stage, we should be able to choose our design risk more logically and perhaps cautiously to change our conventions of risk analysis.

M. J. HAMLIN AND C. E. WRIGHT. We are grateful to Mr Rydz for putting the paper into the context of both design and operation. The distinction between designing with an assumption of foresight and operating without it is an important one and one of which we were very conscious in preparing the paper. As stated in our conclusions the fact that the drought ended in August and did not persist through to the end of November has had a significant influence on return periods and is a feature which is distinctly different from the earlier droughts with which the 1975–76 drought has been compared.

H. B. JACKSON (*Central Water Planning Unit, Reading, U.K.*). The analyses of Professor Hamlin and Mr Wright were limited to clean-water rivers – those used for public water supply – and used naturalized river flow data. Was any consideration given to studying the more industrial rivers (looking at actual flows) bearing in mind that the artificial component of flow is in many cases also a function of the drought severity?

M. J. HAMLIN AND C. E. WRIGHT. A long flow record of, say, 40 or 50 years is essential for the type of analyses we have presented. We do not have access to, nor do we know of, such long records for industrial rivers and were therefore unable to include them in the paper.

R. G. SHARPE (*Severn–Trent Water Authority, U.K.*). I feel that there is a need for further examination of the fact that 1975–76 flows were much less extreme events than those assessed for rainfall. Acknowledging that there is not a direct relation between rainfall and run-off, it nonetheless seems remarkable and difficult to explain that runoff deficit was less severe than rainfall deficit, particularly in 1976. The antecedent dry weather in the late summer of 1975 and winter of 1975–76, coupled with conditions conducive to high evaporation in the hot summer of 1976, would suggest that flow deficits would have been even more extreme than rainfall deficits rather than the reverse. Yet it is clear from table 4 in respect of the Thames Catchment, and figure 6 relating to the River Severn, that 1976 was only the third or fourth most severe year this century for river flows for periods of drought of critical significance for most water resources, i.e. dry weather of 3 or more consecutive months. Indeed, there have been 3 more severe years of cumulative low flow in the past 56 years.

Antecedent rainfall before these earlier droughts this century, notably 1921 and 1933–34, were average or above and greater than that of 1975–76 which was preceded by a series of winters drier than average. Furthermore, it is inconceivable that evaporative conditions were markedly greater in these earlier years compared with 1976.

An explanation for the reason why run-off stood up so relatively well to the exceptional rainfall shortage would be interesting and useful for the future.

M. J. HAMLIN AND C. E. WRIGHT. The problem of relating frequency of occurrence of rainfall deficiencies to that of riverflows has been highlighted by Mr Sharp. He makes some interesting points that required careful consideration. The probabilities of the run-off and of the rainfall event are different because run-off is a function of both current and antecedent rainfall. Thus, from table 7 in the paper, if the rainfall for August in the Thames basin was 5.4 mm it would correspond to the 1 % probability event. However, the riverflow would be little affected by the August rainfall alone, being heavily dependent on the previous 16 months rain. Hence the actual riverflow and therefore its probability of occurrence could vary over a very wide range. This effect becomes less dramatic as the period of shortage being considered increases.

The tables and figures in the paper underline this essential difference between the probabilities of occurrence of the two features of the drought and it is necessary to state that there is no reason to suppose that our river gauging and rainfall records are inconsistent to the extent that they have masked the true severity of the 1975–76 drought. This is substantiated by the analysis of river flows generated by catchment models for the rivers Severn and Thames for the notable droughts of 1921, 1933–34 and 1975–76.

The problems therefore lie in the start and end conditions of the droughts, the effect of evaporation and the lagged effect of antecedent weather conditions. We believe that these factors fully substantiate the fact that the 1976 low flows over the longer durations were not as severe as the corresponding rainfall events. In the Severn catchment to Bewdley, the winters of 1932–33 and 1933–34 were substantially drier than 1974–75 and 1975–76, in terms of the positive increments of rainfall less evaporation. This has been estimated as:

1932–33, 296 mm; 1974–75, 469 mm;
1933–34, 110 mm; 1975–76, 177 mm.

Also, the drought terminated earlier in 1976 than it did in 1934. These two factors combined to ensure that the minimum cumulative flows for the longer durations, such as 9 months, were significantly smaller in 1933–34 than in 1975–76.

In the Thames catchment to Teddington similar features may be discerned. The winter of 1974–75 was appreciably wetter than 1932–33. The positive increments of rainfall less evaporation for these winters has been estimated as:

1932–33, 279 mm; 1974–75, 422 mm;
1933–34, 12 mm; 1975–76, 0 mm.

In this catchment too the drought terminated earlier in 1976 than it did in 1934. Groundwater levels and spring flows were relatively high in both catchments in April 1975 compared with April 1933.

The effects of antecedent rainfall less actual evaporation should be considered, rather than antecedent rainfall alone as quoted by Mr Sharp. Although potential evaporation was very high in the hot summer of 1976, actual evaporation by August was generally low, owing to the exceptionally high soil moisture deficit that already existed. In 1921 the very dry summer was followed by a dry autumn, which resulted in exceptionally low flows persisting into the winter months. This was particularly marked in the Thames catchment and is the reason why the 9 month minimum flows at Teddington for 1921 are lower than any other this century. The early termination of the drought in 1976, due to heavy rainfall in September and October, was a major reason why water resources were not more severely tested. Table 10 shows that flows in the river Thames started to rise 2 or 3 months earlier in 1976 compared with the two earlier events.

TABLE 10. MEAN MONTHLY FLOWS (cubic metres per second) FOR THE RIVER THAMES TO TEDDINGTON FOR THE YEARS 1921, 1934 AND 1976

year	Aug.	Sept.	Oct.	Nov.	Dec.
1921	12.0	14.7	15.2	17.8	22.5
1934	13.2	13.9	15.1	21.7	109.5
1976	10.0	20.6	56.8	80.2	157.7

Proc. R. Soc. Lond. A. **363**, 97–107 (1978)

Printed in Great Britain

Pollution problems arising from the 1975–76 drought

By A. W. Davies

*Anglian Water Authority, Diploma House, Grammar School Walk,
Huntingdon PE18 6NZ, U.K.*

The paper considers the gradual transition from the 'normal' quality state of surface and ground waters and discusses the rapid change in the quality of these waters with the onset of heavy rain towards the end of August 1976.

Many activities within the hydrological cycle were affected directly and indirectly by the drought, as for example treatment of sewage, of water for supply, accelerated eutrophication of reservoirs, and river waters and of fisheries. The degree to which these were influenced by the changing quality and diminishing water quantity resources is described.

Some of the work carried out to alleviate and reduce the impact of the drought on water quantity and quality resources is mentioned and the problems which continue to affect the operations of regional water authorities into the present year as a result of the drought are referred to.

Introduction

The 1975–76 drought was exceptional. Within it, measured rainfall over England and Wales showed large variations, from 50 % of the long-term average for the Midlands and South to 80 % for East Anglia and the North.

Long-term averages can be deceptive as they tend to 'even out' exceptional events; indeed, if the annual average precipitation is taken January–December 1976, it is only 44 mm short of a 'normal' year in Cambridgeshire.

It was apparent in February 1976 that a dry summer would lead to difficulties, with water levels in underground and surface waters considerably depleted, and with little or no recharge during the winter 1975–76. In defence, however, the intensity and duration of the drought could not have been anticipated.

The drought was a considerable test to the newly created Regional Water Authorities and it is confidently stated that the impact of the drought on public industry and agricultural activities would have been more severe had not these authorities been operational.

The appearance of effects of the drought on the quality of surface and ground waters was surprisingly slow, not becoming apparent until the end of July 1976. After the onset of heavy rain toward the end of August 1976, the quality of both surface and ground waters began to rapidly deteriorate early in November. This quality change was primarily related to increasing concentrations of nitrate and sulphate in surface and ground waters; in the latter, response was much slower and it is thought that for some geological formations the peak may not be reached until mid-1978.

[97]

Many of the problems encountered during the drought of 1975–76 occur in a normal year; however, during the period described, these problems were considerably accentuated.

In the context of this paper, pollution is regarded as any activity, whether artificial or natural, that results in a measurable deterioration in water quality to the detriment of the user.

The paper is divided into two principal parts: drought period, and immediate post-drought period. Various aspects of pollution are dealt with under each head, but the subject is so closely interrelated that some repetition is inevitable.

DROUGHT PERIOD

Sewerage and sewage treatment

General

The efficiency of treating sewage is measured by the quality of the final effluent produced, usually in terms of compliance to quality consent limits of biochemical oxygen demand, suspended solids and, in some instances, ammoniacal nitrogen.

Many factors influence the efficiency of a treatment works, the more important being the strength and volume of the influent, air temperature and rainfall intensity and duration. In the Anglian region, as in many other parts of the country, the compliance of sewage effluents to quality conditions improved during the drought by at least 5 % when compared with the same period of the previous year, due mainly to a reduction in sewage flows and higher temperatures. This overall improvement in sewage treatment during the middle months of the drought was reflected in the quality of certain receiving rivers; a most important factor when, during the drought, the volume of sewage effluent in one of these was 80 % of the river flow, which comprised an important source of water for domestic and industrial use.

The drought, however, did create many problems at individual works, and these are briefly described below.

Flows

A very marked reduction in flows to sewage treatment works was general for the country when compared with the same period of the previous year: for example, the Northampton sewage treatment works received 40 % less flow than in the corresponding period in 1975. Such flow reductions were attributed to water saving by industry and the general public and a gradual reduction of infiltration into the sewerage system from groundwater. These smaller flows increased retention times at overloaded sewage treatment works but, combined with the high temperatures, caused problems of septicity at underloaded works. The increased retention of sewage in the sewerage system meant that many sewers functioned as sedimentation tanks, resulting in a large increase in complaints about the smell from rising mains and pumping stations etc. These problems were tackled with the use of hydrogen peroxide, lime, oxygen and chlorine and also with aerial masking chemicals. Many blockages occurred after heavy rainfall at pumping stations and at the coarse screens at the inlet of sewage treatment works and in sewers. Generally no serious damage to sewers occurred except in isolated instances when drying out caused ground movement.

As a result of decreased flow, crude sewages were stronger, i.e. they possessed more biochemical oxygen demand and suspended solids per unit volume but the load remained constant; however, where deposition was occurring in the sewers, the pollution load to the works was also reduced. The flows to many small sewage works ceased for long periods, particularly at night time, which resulted in problems with the dosing rate on the percolating filters and in the management of activated sludge plants due to the development of abnormal sludge characteristics. Such problems were partly alleviated by introducing temporary re-circulation of treated effluent at the works.

Temperature

The effect of high temperature was to decrease the amount of dissolved oxygen that could be introduced into activated sludge and also to dry out the surface of many percolating filters, resulting in the death of the organisms responsible for oxidizing organic matter.

Although nitrification occurred at several works for the first time on record, many works suffered from denitrification in final sedimentation tanks, resulting in problems of rising sludge caused by entrapped nitrogen released in this process.

Where land irrigation was used as a form of tertiary treatment, evaporation of the effluent on the grass plots often resulted in the complete cessation of discharge for long periods.

Prolific growths of algae in sewage lagoons caused an apparent deterioration in terms of suspended solids in the qualities of these effluents discharged to rivers. The high air temperatures shortened the drying periods for sludge in sludge drying beds, and the demands from agriculture for wet sludges substantially increased; from 1 April to 30 September 1976, 66 % of all sludges produced in the Anglian region were disposed to agricultural land, 75 % of which was as wet sludge. Furthermore, the quantities of cess pool and septic tank liquors disposed to sewage treatment works diminished considerably and, in some places, ceased altogether; this was reflected particularly in decreased sludge production. In the Norwich Sewage Division this amounted to a reduction of 15 %.

One of the most important factors affecting the quality of river waters, in spite of rapidly decreasing river flow, was the absence of storm sewage discharges; the influence of these will be considered under Rivers, p. 102.

Water supply

General

The physical, chemical and bacteriological quality of water supplies in the Anglian region is assessed in relation to the World Health Organisation (W.H.O.) *European standards* (1970) *for drinking water.*

The major effects of the drought on the quality of raw waters were the development of extensive algal blooms and animal infestations within reservoirs and river systems, the deterioration in the fabric of the distribution systems and a general increase in the organic content and concentration of conservative substances such as chloride in surface waters. The groundwater quality remained relatively unchanged and the nitrate concentrations in both ground and surface waters showed their normal seasonal decrease.

Problems of increasing nitrate and sulphate concentrations were, however, expected from surface water run-off and groundwater recharge after the drought and the quality of alternative sources for emergency use gave rise to some concern, in particular those possessing high natural fluoride and chloride levels.

There was a marked increase during the drought of complaints relating to discoloration, which was directly attributed to the shortage of water available for flushing mains. In a few areas within the region, particularly those served by the Ardleigh Reservoir, taste and odour problems were experienced by consumers.

Bacteria

The bacteriological quality of water treated for domestic supply was very good during the drought period; no deterioration was measured in raw waters whether from reservoir or direct abstraction from rivers or groundwater.

Algae

The development of algal blooms is a characteristic of waters containing large concentrations of nutrients and such waters are said to be eutrophicated. The nutrients mainly responsible are phosphorus, nitrates, iron, vitamin B_1 and silica. The main source of phosphorus in eutrophicated waters is thought to be sewage treatment works, and that of nitrates agricultural run-off. In the Anglian region, reservoirs and those rivers that are used for public water supplies may be regarded as eutrophic impoundments.

Algal blooms take many different forms, ranging from the green to the blue-green and it is not uncommon for several algae to be present in very large numbers within any one algal bloom, although it is usual to have a dominant species. As early as January–March 1976, considerable blooms were being reported from several water storage reservoirs in the Anglian region: as examples, in Ardleigh and Covenham reservoirs during late February, *Aphanizomenon* blooms increased very rapidly, and at the end of March there had developed in Grafham Reservoir a substantial bloom of *Stephanodiscus*. This organism was considered responsible for an increase in the turbidity of the final water after treatment, which was also accompanied by a marginal increase in the residual iron concentration. At this time, in a report prepared for the Anglian Water Authority, it was stated that '...the continuance of the drought could cause excessive algal blooms in eutrophic impoundments in the region during the summer and autumn period'. Indeed, severe treatment problems were experienced on Ardleigh, Grafham, Covenham and Foxcote reservoirs as early as April 1976; the latter had to be closed towards the end of April as considerable blockage of the filter system and unacceptably large iron and turbidity residuals were entering the final treated water. By July, both Grafham and Ardleigh were affected by severe blooms of *Microcystis*. In both the normal treatment was found to be incompatible with removing the offending bloom and the breakdown products that resulted. At Grafham, alum treatment was introduced without soda softening and this gave substantial improvement in the final water but turbidity residuals were still above average. *Microcystis* blooms were also known to have occurred at approximately the same time in the reservoirs of the Thames Water Authority. The general result of intense algal activity is to produce, on boiling, an earthy taste and musty odour in the treated water; the iron and turbidity content increases and, with the alga *Microcystis*, acidification of the final water produces a cotton-wool type floc caused by mucopolysaccharides; manufacturers of soft drinks were in some difficulties.

The reservoirs at Pitsford and Ardleigh were both subject to severe stratification and, to prevent the deterioration in raw water quality, air injection systems were introduced and successfully mixed the reservoirs.

To demonstrate the density of unicellular algal cells, a sample taken from the Revesby Reservoir is given as an example. At the maximum development 230000 cells/ml were recorded, of which 75000 were *Chlorella*, 75000 *Scenedesmus*, 20000 *Navicula*, 60000 small centric diatoms; in addition to this, 50000 green flagellates/ml were recorded. This density of algal cells was reflected in a maximum figure of 70 µg/l of chlorophyll *a*, with mean levels of 57 µg/l; a 'normal' level is 10 µg/l. The maximum chlorophyll *a* recorded in the final treated water leaving the Revesby treatment plant was 0.7 µg/l.

To remove the earthy type odours and unacceptable tastes, activated carbon treatment was used and while this had some success at Grafham Water, it failed at Ardleigh.

Chemical

Despite the severe drought the quality of water derived from direct river abstractions within the region was reported to have been satisfactory.

At the Clapham intake (River Great Ouse), however, it was found necessary towards the end of the drought to limit river abstraction, because of difficulties in treating the increased algal concentrations in the river, and the large chloride content, which, for the first time, exceeded 100 mg/l (as Cl^-). Similar increases occurred in the River Stour in Essex and for the most part were caused by the increasing proportion of sewage effluent discharging to the river, compared with the diminishing flow from groundwater sources. As previously mentioned, the nitrate concentration in both surface and groundwaters reflected the normal decrease expected during summer months. However, a rapid rise in nitrate concentrations in both ground and surface waters was expected, as nitrates normally increase in the autumn and spring of each year because of land drainage run-off and ground-water recharge. Taking into account the relatively higher nitrate concentration in some ground and surface waters as a result of the drought, i.e. between 11.3 and 22.6 mg/l nitrate nitrogen, $(NO_3)N$, consideration of remedial options was given a high priority. (The nitrate nitrogen concentrations of 11.3 and 22.6 mg/l correspond to the recommended and acceptable levels defined in the W.H.O. *European standards* (1970).)

Two bottling plants were installed: one in Lincolnshire, the other in Ipswich, to supply bottled water to households with infants that might need it. Above 22.6 mg/l nitrate, the susceptibility of infants to methaemoglobinaemia (blue-baby) is increased. Work was also initiated on the construction of two deionization plants and the planning of an experimental denitrification plant.

To utilize many different sources of water possessing different qualities, which replaced what was under normal circumstances a single source, it was necessary to carry out many investigations to assess the need for increased or changed water treatment. This applied particularly to industrial users, where the effect of quality changes on their manufacturing processes could be substantial, i.e. boiler feed water, softening plant, etc. The biggest difficulty was with the total dissolved solid content of the various sources.

One of the more difficult prediction exercises on likely changes in water quality arose in the project on the Reversal of Direction of the Ely Ouse (Rodeo). (See below, p. 104.)

Rivers

General

The low river flows that had characterized the summer of 1975 continued throughout the winter of 1975–76 leading to several problems not experienced during the summer months. Most notable of these was the marked increase in ammonia in those rivers whose flows were largely of sewage effluents. The reason for this was the lower ambient temperature during the winter reducing the nitrification rate in sewage works and also in the rivers. This situation created problems at water treatment works, particularly in maintaining an optimum level of residual chlorine.

As with the water storage reservoirs, when the temperatures rose in the spring, ammonia content decreased but algal blooms began to develop at the beginning of March 1976, at least two months earlier than would be expected under normal spring flow conditions.

From April 1976 onwards, river temperatures increased and a temperature of 30 °C was not an infrequent occurrence. Algal activity was also very great, leading to day-time levels of dissolved oxygen up to 410 % saturation accompanied by pH values in excess of 8, both resulting from the intense photosynthetic activity. Numerous fish mortalities were associated with these conditions; 20 such incidents occurred in the catchments of the Welland, Nene and Great Ouse in the months May–July 1976.

As river flows continued to diminish, severe saline incursions occurred in the lower reaches of many rivers in Anglia. The primary concern was that water used for spray irrigation, particularly in the Fenlands, would be rendered unusable at a time when spray irrigation demands were at a maximum; the large chloride content might be detrimental to livestock drinking from rivers, and even to fish. Very few fish mortalities were in fact attributed to chloride. Many cattle were, however, affected by saline poisoning and one died. These incidents occurred in the Wash Counter Drain/Old Bedford River and on the Bure Marshes in Norfolk. Monitoring programmes were established and analysis of waters was undertaken for farmers. Efforts were also made to minimize the ingress of saline water at tidal sluices and, wherever possible, fresh water was released to displace saline water in the lower reaches; the ability to control the situation in this way was very limited. In spite of the increased river flows in September, high chloride levels persisted until the beginning of October 1976.

Serious deterioration in water quality in many rivers occurred for short periods during the drought when heavy rainfall, associated with storm activity, resulted in large polluting loads entering rivers from urban run-off, and the discharge of storm sewage. These organic loads were mainly attributed to extensive deposition of detritus in the sewers that were flushed by the storm water. This detritus also blocked coarse screens at sewage treatment works, pumping stations and in sewers, resulting in flooding. The primary effect of these high organic loads of short duration was to severely deoxygenate the receiving river. To ameliorate the more severe areas of deoxygenation, artificial aeration was carried out using surface aerators and pure oxygen, with limited success.

The net effect during the drought was that river water quality remained better than expected; this is particularly surprising when the low dilution afforded to sewage discharges is considered. The explanation is thought to be a combination of high water temperature and algal activity, which substantially increased the self-purification capability of the rivers, particularly in the months of May, June and July. Furthermore, the increased retention time in the river, as a result of low river velocity, meant that the impact of measured pollution from sewage effluents was considerably diminished in terms of distance from the outfall.

While self-purification effects the recovery of river quality from biodegradable pollutants, it does not alter the concentration of conservative or non-biodegradable substances such as chloride and sulphate. The only practicable method of lowering the concentration of such substances is by dilution or removal at source. Towards the end of the drought period, even in the absence of salt water incursion, some rivers contained chloride concentrations in excess of 150 mg/l and sulphates above 200 mg/l; these concentrations were the highest recorded during low river flows. The 'normal' concentrations for these constituents in these rivers during the summer are 100 mg/l chloride and 150 mg/l sulphate. The primary reason for these significant increases was inadequate river dilution relative to industrial discharges and sewage effluents.

Rodeo Project

The project involved raising 15 million gallons per day over seven locks on the lower Bedford Ouse (a total difference in height of some 9 m) and thereby augmenting with Ely Ouse water the quantity available for abstraction into Grafham Water Reservoir. Before the operation of the scheme it was necessary to take several steps to protect water quality. A dam was built across the tidal New Bedford River to prevent saline water being drawn into the system, and a new pipeline was constructed to supply the Huntingdon area with water from Grafham, thus allowing the direct abstraction from the river at Brampton to be terminated. Special attention was given to improving and maintaining the quality of effluents from key sewage treatment works discharging to the catchment of the scheme. At Kings Lynn it was necessary to effect a 50 % reduction in polluting load by chemically aided treatment because of the reduction in dilution for this discharge that resulted from the scheme. Surveys were made of industrial discharges to the catchment of the Rodeo scheme, and in three instances it was necessary for industrialists to reduce the polluting loads discharged. Special chemical and biological surveys were mounted before and during the operation of the scheme.

Operation of the scheme began early in October but was discontinued after only three weeks owing to the heavy and persistent rainfall in September and October. As at other times throughout the drought, the Authority had to apply to the Department of the Environment for a drought order to carry out this work, and had to submit evidence on water quality aspects.

Fisheries

The occurrence of fish mortalities during the drought has already been mentioned. Mortalities were reported from all parts of the country and were attributed variously to high temperature, heavy growth of algae and other aquatic plants, lack of water (some enclosed waters dried up completely), salt water incursion, the discharge of storm sewage and run-off, and increased poaching. It is estimated that some 250 000 fish died as a result of the exceptional conditions in natural watercourses in the Anglian Water Authority region during the drought. In addition, 10 t of table trout, $1\frac{1}{4}$ t of brood fish and 300 000 fry were lost at a Lincolnshire fish farm as a result of excessively high water temperature.

There were very few adverse effects upon the spawning of coarse fish and, indeed, it was concluded that 1976 was a particularly good spawning year. River flows had risen again before the time of trout spawning, although doubts have been expressed about the survival of the previous year's fry in the low spring flows experienced in some areas.

The small freshwater flows failed to attract migrating salmon and sea-trout into the rivers, and fish passes failed to operate properly. The consequent concentration of fish in estuaries led to serious poaching problems and the deaths of many salmon were reported in some estuaries. Despite the losses, angling catches of coarse fish remained good throughout most of the drought period and it has been suggested that the warmer conditions led to an increase in the feeding activity of fish. Because of low water levels there were difficulties of access on reservoir trout fisheries, but catches were nevertheless comparable with those of previous years. Salmon catches from rivers were substantially smaller, probably because of the problems of migration referred to above, and in some rivers they were only 50 % of the long-term average catch.

POST-DROUGHT PERIOD: SEPTEMBER TO DECEMBER 1976

General

The problems of water quality associated with the drought continued into early October in spite of the heavy rainfall experienced during September. By the latter part of October, however, the salt waters which had penetrated many rivers had receded to their normal position.

With the onset of heavy rain at the beginning of September, many pollutions occurred, principally from surface water run-off and storm sewage discharges. The effect of these discharges, with a die-back in algal blooms and cooler river water, caused severe deoxygenation resulting in some fish kills. However, the impact on the quality of rivers after heavy rainfall immediately following the drought was not as great as expected. This is mainly attributed to rapidly increasing river flows which afforded dilution to these discharges. There was a progressive improvement in the biochemical oxygen demand and dissolved oxygen during October and November as the quality of storm water improved and the effects of decaying plant material declined.

The performance of sewage treatment plants was sustained after the drought; this was to some extent unexpected. The improvement noted during the summer, attributed to the hot, dry weather, was expected to decline during the wetter, colder months. One of the major factors was that the sewage loads to treatment plants were smaller at high flows because storm sewages were being discharged from pumping stations, sewers and sewage treatment works.

The most notable change in the quality of river water during the period was the rapid increase in the concentration of nitrates, particularly in surface waters throughout the region. The nitrate concentrations began to rise in early October and were maintained until *March 1977*, and then began to fall generally. As a result of the increase, it was necessary to restrict the quantities of water abstracted directly from rivers for public water supply and to supplement from other sources. The nitrate concentrations were some of the largest ever measured in the United Kingdom: one river reached 40 mg/l nitrate nitrogen, while concentrations between 20 and 25 mg/l were not uncommon.

There was not, in general, the same dramatic rise in nitrate concentrations in groundwater, although similar effects may appear in due course. However, some localized increases have occurred, notably in the highly fissured limestone of South Lincolnshire.

The large increase in nitrate concentrations in rivers is attributable to several factors associated with the drought of 1976. The effect was remarkable in that the high concentrations occurred at times of high river flow; the total quantity of nitrate nitrogen in the rivers was therefore extremely large and the nitrate levels were sustained for a very long time. This suggests that the relatively constant input from sewage treatment works was making only a minor contribution to the total and that the major share must have been derived from land drainage waters. The shortage of summer rain during 1976 limited nitrogen uptake by crops because the soil was dry, and high temperature increased nitrogen fixation in the soil. Subsequently, winter rainfall leached this nitrogen from the soil.

In some waters, high concentrations of sulphate probably came from land drains, but on the River Nene mine water discharges made a substantial contribution.

The effect of the drought was to draw down reservoirs to dangerously low levels; indeed the Rodeo scheme was designed to provide additional water to sustain Grafham Reservoir as a useful source of potable supply. On the onset of rainfall, considerable emphasis was placed upon pumping all water thereby made available into the reservoirs. The poor quality was later to prove a constraint to further pumping, particularly into Rutland Water. Between 1 October 1976 and 31 March 1977 the volume of water stored in the new Rutland Water reservoir increased from 3740×10^6 to 25156×10^6 gallons (from 17000 to 114360 Ml). Of the water added, 29 % was pumped from the River Nene, 35 % from the River Welland and 36 % was derived from the natural catchment of Rutland Water.

During the last three months of 1976 marked changes took place in the quality of water in the reservoir as a result of the large quantities of water added. Nitrate concentrations rose from 1.1 to 10.6 mg/l as $(NO_3)N$ and sulphates from 125 to more than 200 mg/l. Increases also occurred in the concentrations of silica, calcium and dissolved phosphate. Chloride concentrations fell slightly and the growth of algae also declined during this period.

In late December it was necessary to cease pumping water from the River Nene as the concentration of sulphate in both the Nene and the reservoir exceeded 200 mg/l, and although the concentration fell in January 1977, no further abstraction was possible until *March 1977* because the nitrates in the river had reached more than 15 mg/l as $(NO_3)N$. Use of the River Welland was also curtailed for a week in early January because of large nitrate concentrations.

The careful monitoring of the quality of water pumped into the reservoir was necessary because the rapid programme of filling gave little opportunity for self-purification before its use for supply through the treatment works, which began in February 1977. Under normal circumstances, the quality of the stored water would have been substantially improved had the minimum retention time of six months been available for the pumped water. Improvement could also have been expected for this water by dilution.

Problems can be expected in future years as a result of the extremely poor quality water that was pumped into reservoirs such as Grafham, Rutland and Pitsford during and after the drought. Organic matter and nitrate will be the main sources of trouble.

Conclusions

By the end of March 1977 the principal effects of the drought on river water quality had passed and conditions were close to 'normal' for that time of year. The long-term effects of using poor quality water to fill water supply reservoirs cannot be predicted accurately, but it is expected that these waters will present greater treatment difficulties in meeting water supply quality criteria in the future.

The effect on groundwater quality may not become apparent for some time. This is particularly so for water abstracted from chalk. The nitrate levels in limestone and gravel waters appear, at the time of writing (September 1977), to have reached the maximum and be decreasing, although some upturn is to be expected on the recharge of these aquifers during the forthcoming winter. It appears unlikely that the problems experienced during the post-drought period will recur unless a very dry summer is followed by an equally wet winter. The effect of the drought on the nitrate levels, particularly in groundwater, was to enhance the upward trend, which evidence available suggests commenced in the early 1950s.

In retrospect, had not the drought been followed by very heavy rain, the problems of post-drought quality would have been more severe. The largest single factor which reduced the impact of post-drought pollution was dilution.

My thanks are due to the Chairman of the Anglian Water Authority for his encouragement in the writing of this paper and also to the staff and colleagues who have assisted.

Proc. R. Soc. Lond. A. **363**, 109–130 (1978)

Printed in Great Britain

Planning for development of groundwater and surface water resources

By O. Gibb and H. J. Richards

Central Water Planning Unit, Reading Bridge House, Reading, RG1 8PS, U.K.

The assessment and development of water resources are considered in relation to present demands and the developed and potential water resources of England and Wales. Normal seasonal changes in storage are compared with those of 1975–76 and conditions during this period compared with previous droughts.

Problems that arose in the summer of 1976 are considered together with the measures taken by water authorities to overcome local shortages. The implications of the shortages are considered in relation to methods of determining and defining the reliability of supplies. Criteria for planning the future development of water resources are discussed in the light of conclusions drawn from the 1975–76 drought and in relation to general planning considerations.

There is no basic shortage of water and the extent of restrictions which may have to be applied during drought events is largely determined by the price the consumer is prepared to pay for the safeguard of additional capacity and assured supply.

Introduction

The 1975–76 drought, which affected the whole of England and Wales to a greater or lesser extent and Scotland and Ireland hardly at all, is now recognized as having started in May 1975. This was just one year after the major reorganization of the water industry in England and Wales under the Water Act of 1973. That Act created, on 1 April 1974, nine Regional Water Authorities in England and one in Wales with responsibilities in whole river basins, or groups of basins, for water conservation and water supply, sewerage and sewage disposal, pollution control, fisheries, land drainage, recreation and amenity. The objective of the Act was to create authorities with the statutory responsibilities and powers to undertake comprehensive river basin planning and management. The main benefits foreseen were the consideration by the one responsible authority of water quantity and water quality and supply problems and the integration of previously fragmented, independent authorities within natural river basins, to facilitate the development and deployment of water resources over wider areas than had been possible in the past. The boundaries of the water authority areas are indicated in figure 1.

Planning for water resource developments is a long-term process, and schemes may take upwards of ten years to mature from first conception. It could not be

FIGURE 1. Boundaries of water authority areas in England and Wales.
Land areas over 244 m are stippled.

expected, therefore, that the new water authorities would have had time to influence to any degree the pattern in their areas. They were faced with the situation that arose in 1975, with the assets inherited from their predecessors, but with the one important difference: that they had the ability to deploy those resources more flexibly over wider areas to meet problems of acute shortages and to introduce new emergency sources with much greater facility than their predecessors. Their main constraint was the extent of engineering works that it was practicable to undertake under the emergency conditions that prevailed.

Resources

Water resources are available from that part of rainfall not returned to the atmosphere by evaporation or used to overcome any existing soil moisture deficit. This residual rainfall is thus available to run off into surface water bodies or to infiltrate to replenish storage in aquifers. It is customary to define available resources as the average annual run-off, or residual rainfall, over a long time-scale. The average annual rainfall over England and Wales is 904 mm, based on the standard period 1916–50. Other standard periods have been used but this is the most recent based on numerous and reliable records, although averages for

TABLE 1. WATER RESOURCES IN ENGLAND AND WALES
(thousands of cubic metres per day)

regional water authority	average annual run-off	minimum daily run-off averaged over driest month	daily yield of existing and authorized sources	total groundwater resource	groundwater abstraction in 1975
North West	33 200	3 300	2 000	2 200	641
Northumbrian	12 800	900	1 100	2 300	96
Severn–Trent	19 000	1 500	3 100	3 300	1 126
Yorkshire	17 700	1 100	1 300	4 300	325
Anglian	9 200	1 000	1 800	1 300	964
Thames	8 300	1 100	3 500	4 100	1 729
Southern	9 300	1 800	1 500	3 600	1 030
Wessex	10 800	2 100	900	3 800	353
South West	21 500	2 200	400	400	128
Welsh	49 600	5 100	2 400	1 500	175
total	**190 000**	**20 000**	**18 000**	**30 800**	**6 567**

the shorter period are also available and are now used (Central Water Planning Unit 1977*a*). Based on the 1916–50 data and estimating losses for evaporation, the average annual run-off is equivalent to 460 mm of residual rainfall or about 190×10^6 m³/d. By comparison, present public water supply consumption is 15×10^6 m³/d – approximately 8 % of available resources. Agriculture uses an additional 0.37×10^6 m³/d for irrigation, which represents a complete loss; and industry, including C.E.G.B., uses a massive 27×10^6 m³/d, mainly for cooling, but about 95 % of this is returned close to source and, apart from changes in quality, has little impact on total available resources (Water Resources Board 1974). The pattern varies considerably regionally. Total water resources have been summarized in a report by the Water Resources Board (1973) and the details of surface water resources in table 1 have been obtained from that report. The summary of groundwater resources is based on a provisional assessment by the Central Water Planning Unit. These totals are approximate and are subject to the review which each water authority is currently undertaking as required under the terms of Section 24(6) of the Water Act 1973.

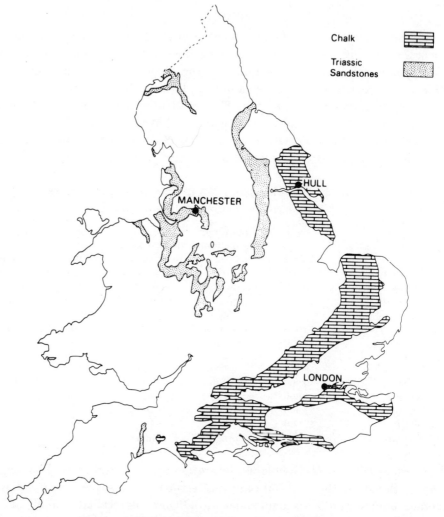

FIGURE 2. Major aquifers in England and Wales.

Because of the seasonal and annual variability of rainfall and, more important, high evaporation losses in summer, actual river flows can decrease to less than 10 % of average. These small flows are normally considered just adequate to maintain the health of our rivers. Thus if continuous supplies are to be maintained, storage has to be provided or developed from which supplies can be drawn when natural run-off falls below that needed to maintain the supply and the minimum flow required in rivers.

Storage takes one of two forms: reservoirs used traditionally to supplement surface run-off either by direct supply or more recently by river regulation, or storage in aquifers developed in the course of pumping from wells and boreholes. Water stored in aquifers can be utilized in much the same way as that in a surface reservoir. Groundwater provides 25 % of the total volume of water used in England and Wales, if the requirements for thermal power generation are excluded, and 34 % of public water supply. Figure 2 shows the distribution of the major aquifers in England and Wales.

Our available fresh water resources provide a sufficient quantity to meet foreseeable needs, but only if provision is made for necessary storage and transfers of water to ensure continuation of supply during dry periods, such provision adding to the considerable services built up over the past 150 years. One of the problems of water resource planning is the determination of how much storage to provide for such dry periods, keeping in mind the problems of the reliability of hydrological records, understanding of the relevant parts of the hydrological cycle, the degree of reliability of supplies to be ensured and the economic factors influencing the water industry.

Residual rainfall varies geographically and seasonally. 'Seasonal evaporation' reaches a maximum in the summer months and is generally almost negligible during winter. Soil moisture deficits increase during warm dry weather and rain is needed in excess of the evaporation rate in order to overcome the deficit and bring the soil to field capacity before providing residual rainfall sufficient to allow surface run-off and infiltration to the water table.

Estimates of potential resources in upland catchments rely on definition of catchment boundaries and long-term average rainfall and evaporation. The design of a system of storage to utilize available rainfall involves considerations of the volume needed to meet estimated demands to a specified degree of reliability and an analysis of the hydrological information to determine the catchment characteristics. Major engineering works are required to create the dam, reservoir, aqueducts and treatment works, and the storage thus made available can be used for direct supply, river regulation or transfer to another basin.

The design of abstraction systems from groundwater storage relies on the same considerations of demand and analysis of hydrological information. An underground reservoir can be developed in stages, with desk and field studies to evaluate resources, followed by test and production wells to provide the first stage of development. The consequences of development determine the design of subsequent stages. Exploration and aquifer testing well in advance of requirements are needed to ensure efficient and economic development and this was illustrated during the 1976 drought when it was possible, in a number of areas, to drill with confidence new boreholes to help satisfy local water demands.

The 'critical period' for any water storage is the time it will take for storage on or below the surface to reach its lowest level during a dry period. Most surface reservoirs are critical over 6–9 months and some of the larger ones over 18 months. This means that the storage they contain is sufficient to maintain supplies for 9 or 18 months respectively before falling to a level at which they can no longer provide the yield for which they were designed. Before such a stage the operational manager will have introduced measures to reduce demand on the particular reservoir. Most groundwater reservoirs are critical to the conditions during the six winter months in so far as they are recharged or replenished naturally during that time. Normally there is little recharge during the summer months, with exceptions in the north, and so a series of 'dry' winters will result in depletion of groundwater storage.

In some catchments a high level of resource development has already taken place, such as in the Thames, where topography is rather subdued and much of the area is underlain by permeable strata. Flows in such a river basin respond slowly to a drought because groundwater discharge then provides the flow, whereas in a hilly, wet and impermeable catchment such as the Upper Severn or Wye there is a quicker response to, and recovery from, a drought because aquifers do not provide a significant base flow. Regional differences in the level of resource development are indicated in table 1 from which it is seen that the existing and authorized sources make up a small proportion of the average annual run-off in the wetter upland areas of the northwest and southwest. By comparison, the development in the drier lowland areas usually exceeds the minimum daily average and represents a substantial proportion of the average annual run-off. In no authority area are groundwater resources near full development, although in the Anglian Water Authority area the potential for further development is noticeably limited.

THE DRY PERIOD OF 1975–76

During the extreme weather conditions of 1976 there was some general concern as to whether our developed water resources were sufficient to meet demands if the dry period were to continue into the autumn. In the event a 16 month period of rainfall well below average, begininng in May 1975, came to an end during the last few days of August 1976. The provision made by the water industry was severely tested in most areas of England and Wales against the criteria upon which water supply schemes had been designed. Most areas had some form of restriction imposed upon supply, but only in southeast Wales and north Devon were supplies seriously curtailed to domestic users. Supplies to industry were maintained throughout the 'drought', many individual industrial premises making marked savings in the use of water.

The use of the term drought implies to meteorologists in Britain a defined period without measureable rain, and to agriculturalists a shortage of available moisture during the summer growing season as a result of evaporation and transpiration exceeding the total rainfall. A water-supply drought may be defined as any prolonged period of residual rainfall deficiency that results in surface or groundwater sources being unable to maintain the supplies they were designed to provide. Groundwater supplies are affected by deficiencies in the winter half year (October to March) when aquifers are normally replenished. Deficiencies in a single winter or summer will affect surface reservoirs that are expected to empty and refill annually. Combination of two dry summers and an intervening dry winter will affect usually the larger, surface reservoirs that are designed to balance the run-off over a 3 year dry period.

A comparison of the summer and winter rainfall of 1973–74 with the long-term averages for 1916–50 can be seen in table 2. Rainfall over England and Wales was average during the year to March 1975. Examination of the hydrographs in figure 3 indicates that for most months rainfall was near or above average and that this was reflected in river flows and groundwater levels near, or above average. The summer rainfall of that year was 87 % of average whereas during the succeeding winter only 62 % of average fell, so that by 1 April 1976 river flows and groundwater levels were below average, as a result of the residual rainfall deficiency. Despite this, however, the majority of reservoirs were between 75 and 100 % full, only some of the smaller ones, which rely on the rainfall of a single winter, being just over half full.

TABLE 2. SUMMER AND WINTER RAINFALL OVER ENGLAND AND WALES

period	rainfall mm	percentage of average (1916–50)
Oct. 1973 – Mar. 1974	439	90
Apr. 1974 – Sept. 1974	436	101
Oct. 1974 – Mar. 1975	625	106
Apr. 1975 – Sept. 1975	364	87
Oct. 1975 – Mar. 1976	302	62
Apr. 1976 – Sept. 1976†	321	78
Apr. 1976 – Aug. 1976	161	48
Oct. 1976 – Mar. 1977	642	135

† Includes rainfall (210 % of 1916–50 average) of September 1976.

This was followed in turn by the low rainfall of 161 mm between April and August 1976, only 48 % of average for those 5 months. By the end of August, therefore, storage in most reservoirs had been reduced to less than 50 % of the full storage. A single-season reservoir refills naturally in a winter recharge period and allows water to be drawn from the reservoir during the succeeding summer at a specified rate, until the following winter rainfall refills the reservoir. A winter rainfall markedly below the long-term average may not refill the reservoir and during the winter of 1975–76 some of these smaller reservoirs were not refilled by the spring of 1976. These conditions applied to many of the small reservoirs in South Wales and in the Pennines. Other water supply reservoirs were designed to retain in storage sufficient run-off to provide a supply during the three consecutive driest years in a period of 50 or 100 years. During the winter of 1976–77 the rainfall was 135 % of average and by March 1977 had refilled nearly all surface and underground storage.

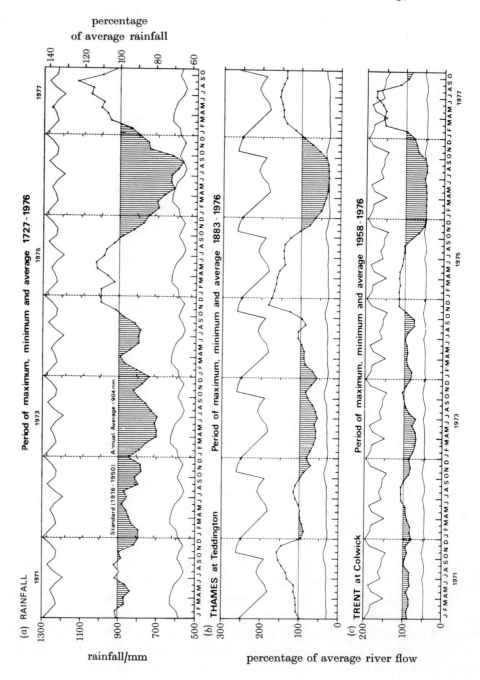

percentage
of average rainfall

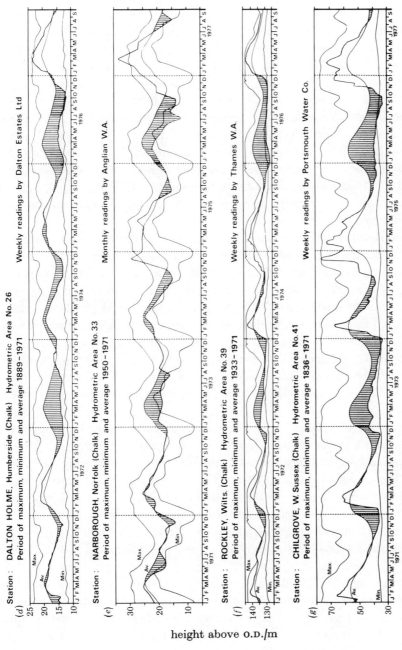

height above o.d./m

FIGURE 3. (*a–c*) Hydrographs of rainfall and river flow, 1971–77. The total average rainfall over England and Wales for the year ending in a particular month is shown by a dot for the end of that month. Shaded areas represent 12 month periods which have been drier than average. In the lower two diagrams shaded areas indicate periods when river flows were below the long-term average. (*d–g*) Hydrographs of groundwater level fluctuation, 1971–77.

COMPARISON WITH PREVIOUS DRY PERIODS

Previous historic droughts have frequently been accepted as the criteria for the design of water supply schemes and those most frequently quoted are the droughts of 1921, 1933–34 and 1959. The dry period of 1921 was significant in the south of England. The south and east also suffered a drought in 1933–34, but neither of these was of much significance in the Midlands and north, whereas in 1959 the north was markedly affected, with very low flows being recorded in the period from June to August in rivers in the north country (Rowntree 1961). A comparison is made in figure 4 of the effects of some selected below-average rainfall periods over England and Wales during this century. Rainfall for the defined drought is shown in each case as a percentage of the long-term average, for February to November 1921 (10 months), April 1933 to September 1934 (18 months), February to November 1964 (10 months) and May 1975 to August 1976 (16 months) (information supplied by the Meteorological Office).

There is no simple relation between the frequency of occurrence of rainfall and river flows or change in groundwater storage, because other important variables are evaporation, soil moisture deficit and infiltration, all of which are dependent on a variety of physical conditions and vary with time. Various types of frequency analysis are used to relate rainfall to particular hydrological problems, and, for seasonal rainfall frequency and projection of river flows, analyses start with data for a specified month. Random starting dates are utilized in looking at general rainfall frequencies and (rainfall minus evaporation) is used to determine residual rainfall, which is required for assessments of water resources, and random starting dates are used in analyses of river flows to derive water resource yields from reservoirs.

The dry summer of 1976 followed a period drier than average beginning in the spring of the previous year, the 16 month period to the end of August 1976 providing an average rainfall over England and Wales of 575 mm, only 64 % of the average for the standard period 1916–50. The probability of such a small rainfall in any 16 month period is of the order of once in 400 years. The probability of such a 16 month period ending in August has been estimated to be likely to occur only about once in a thousand years (Wright 1976). However, care must be exercised in estimating such probabilities, as small percentage differences in total rainfall can change the return period for such a 16 month event from about 1 in 500 to 1 in 1500 years or so. Undoubtedly, over England and Wales the 16 months beginning in May 1975 were the driest since records began in 1727. A comparison between periods in 1975–76 and earlier drought periods is summarized in table 3.

The distribution of the return period for a random start is shown in figure 5, from which it is clear that conditions during 1975–76 were not unusual for a 16 month dry period, starting in any month, in the North West and Northumbrian Water Authority areas; in the extreme southwest and along the east coast similar conditions occur about once in every 20 years. A return period of 1 in 200

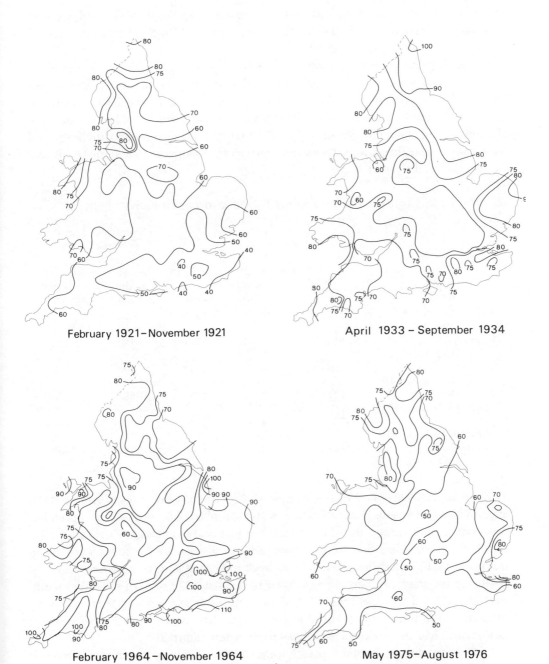

February 1921–November 1921

April 1933 – September 1934

February 1964–November 1964

May 1975–August 1976

FIGURE 4. Percentages of long-term average rainfall for selected droughts over England and Wales (based on Meteorological Office information).

years over most of southern and eastern England and South Wales indicates an unusual occurrence. Along the southern coast from Dorset to Sussex a return period of 1 in 500 years is indicated.

All the historic drought periods obviously do not begin and end in the same months of the year in which they occurred and comparisons are therefore not direct. The dry period 1975–76 ended over England and Wales by the end of August, whereas in 1921 and 1964 the dry weather persisted into the late autumn. If similar conditions had obtained in 1976 many more emergency supplies would have had to be utilized, and it was this concern that exercised the industry during the months of July and August.

TABLE 3. COMPARISON BETWEEN 1975–76 AND PREVIOUS DRY PERIODS

period	rainfall mm	percentage of average (1916–50)	year	previous lowest rainfall/mm (1727–1975) ending August	ending any month
3 months June–Aug. 1976	77	35	1800	74	45
6 months Mar.–Aug. 1976	205	52	1741	184	155
9 months Dec. 1975–Aug. 1976	355	55	1731	400	343
12 months Sept. 1975–Aug. 1976	571	63	1750	608	556
16 months May 1975–Aug. 1976	757	64	1750	809	779
24 months Sept. 1974–Aug. 1976	1497	83	1741	1259	1259

The relatively early end to the drought during the last few days of August 1976 averted further serious restrictions on water supplies. The rainfall in September was double the average and that of October just above average, so that by mid-October soil moisture deficits had been almost satisfied, river flows were rising markedly and groundwater levels were beginning to rise in many areas.

During the very dry period from April to August 1976 rainfall over Wales and western England was less than 40 % of the long term average and there was very little run-off from these impermeable areas, with little or no groundwater storage; as a result river flows decreased markedly in a few months.

In 1976 river flows in many places were smaller than any previously recorded, but the succeeding wet autumn and winter caused flows to increase rapidly and in some areas led to flooding in February 1977. In contrast, those rivers draining areas of permeable Chalk were not so rapidly depleted and the low flows in such areas were the cumulation of two dry summers and the intervening dry winter of 1975–76. The shaded areas in the hydrographs of figure 3 indicate that river flows and groundwater levels were below average from the autumn of 1975 until the following autumn.

Infiltration into the main aquifers during the winter of 1975–76 was, in most areas, well under 30 % of the long-term average and the areas most affected were the Chalk outcrops from Lincolnshire to Dorset and the Triassic sandstones of the Midlands. The seasonal changes in Yorkshire and the North and South Downs were not unusual. Because of their high storage coefficient and very large perma-

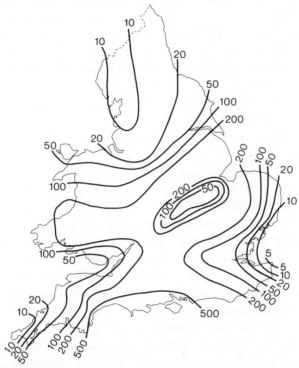

FIGURE 5. Reciprocal of frequency of occurrence of the 16 month dry period of 1975–76 with a start in any month. The lines join areas with a probability of a 16 month period of only 64 % of the long-term average rainfall; thus in northeast Kent a similar situation is likely to arise once in every 5 years, whereas in south Hampshire it is likely only once in 500 years. Information supplied by the Meteorological Office.

nent groundwater storage, the Triassic sandstones were not much affected by a single winter season of rainfall and infiltration below average, or natural recharge. On the whole only wells in upland regions of the Chalk outcrops suffered reduction in yields as a result of extra lowering of groundwater levels in 1976.

Storage in aquifers was not unusually low during the drought of 1976 and any 'failure' of groundwater resources that occurred was a result of lack of well capacity to make use of the storage available.

SHORT-TERM MEASURES

It is appropriate to consider the steps which the industry took during 1975–76 to maintain the public water supply system, because these may have implications for future planning. These measures fall into two categories:

(1) the augmentation of resources;

(2) the restriction of water consumption.

The first is entirely within the control of the water authority, and the second depends in its early, less painful stages, on cooperation from the public.

Augmentation of resources was achieved in a number of ways:

(a) Full exploitation of existing resources by transferring water from areas of surplus to areas of need.

(b) Reducing compensation water flows, or residual flows below abstraction points.

(c) Providing emergency supplies, from sources not previously used or by recommissioning abandoned works.

(d) In some areas by developing a permanent addition to resources from groundwater sources, as was done in the Wessex area.

In parallel with these measures to augment resources, steps were taken to limit water consumption, most of which were facilitated by powers available under the Drought Act (1976). Here there were two clear stages, described in detail in a report on the drought (National Water Council 1977).

The first stage included voluntary savings by consumers as a result of public exhortation, the prohibition of non-essential uses such as hosepipes, garden watering, car washing, pressure reductions and checks on leakage and, in many areas, substantial voluntary reductions in consumption by industry. The precise effect of each of these measures is difficult to assess, but the N.W.C. report quoted savings as great as 30 % in limited areas, with an average approaching 20 % over all the areas badly affected by the drought. Even these savings were not sufficient in the face of dwindling resources in two areas, north Devon and southeast Wales, where the authorities had to proceed to the second stage of rationing supplies. In these circumstances the choice lies between rota cuts or the use of standpipes. The former involves closing the valves on the distribution system so that supplies are only available for certain hours of the day; with the latter normal supplies are cut off at the boundary stopcock, except when this would cause physical hardship, and water has to be obtained from standpipes erected in the streets. Each method has its own operational problems and varying disadvantages for the consumer and the choice may be dictated by the nature of the area. Savings can be increased up to 40 or 45 % although the experience is, fortunately, too limited to provide reliable statistics. Standpipes, by which consumption can be directly controlled, are probably the only alternative in the event of extreme emergency and strict rationing.

The factor of real concern to the water resources planner is the amount by which consumption can be reduced by various voluntary and regulatory measures when an abnormally dry period occurs and the public recognize the need to conserve supplies. Quantification of these savings can provide the basis of a different approach to reliability studies and to planning for a given level of security of supplies.

LONG-TERM PLANNING CONSIDERATIONS

Despite increasing demands, the aggregate of our available freshwater resources is more than adequate to meet our needs provided that storage, transfer, treatment and distribution works are developed to keep pace with rising consumption. The fundamental question for the water resource planner is whether the conditions of 1975–76 indicate the need for a radical change from the standards of reliability that have been accepted as appropriate in the past.

There are two aspects to this question:

1. Do the events of 1975–76 presage a change in climate that necessitates a revision of the historical basis of hydrological assessment?

2. Whatever the basis of hydrological assessment, are the water industry's traditional criteria of 'failure' of a probability of between 1 in 50 or 1 in 100 years adequate and acceptable?

As to the first, all the evidence so far available (Mason 1976) would seem to suggest that 1975–76 was a rare event over England and Wales as a whole in a predominantly random series and that there is no evidence to suggest a significant climatic change within our planning horizon. There has been some speculation on a small decline in average rainfall in the southeast, but nothing to suggest that this is more than a slight variation in the pattern of the past 200 years.

There is a hint of a trend of slightly declining winter rainfall, averaged over about a decade, but no similar trend in total annual rainfall can be seen. The presumption must be that if winter rainfall is declining, summer rainfall must be increasing, albeit that the summer rainfall may be coming in shorter, heavier falls. These 'trends' or variations in annual or seasonal rainfall seem to be evident to some eyes over short periods of a decade or two, but they are placed in their true perspective in a study of rainfall recently completed by the Meteorological Office (Tabony 1977). The translation of minor changes in the balance between summer and winter rainfall, into run-off to reservoirs or recharge to aquifers, is a highly complex business of assessing the actual losses due to evaporation and transpiration, the proportion of run-off that makes good soil moisture deficits and the proportion of the residual that flows into rivers, or infiltrates to recharge aquifers. These processes are still imperfectly understood, despite the large amount of research that has been undertaken in recent years. The conclusion must be that to attempt to take into account the weak trends that appear to have been identified so far could, in the end, lead to much larger errors than an acceptance of the present historical data base.

For the second question, two facts must be recognized:

(a) that given the random variability of the input to water resources, absolute reliability, in terms of a full unrestricted supply at all times, cannot be guaranteed;

(b) that increased reliability can be provided, but only at increased cost and, in the end, the public can be provided only with the standard of reliability that it is prepared to pay for.

The 'reliable yield' of a source has been traditionally defined by water supply engineers as the average quantity of water than can be continuously provided from that source over a dry period likely to occur once or twice in a century and the source is thus said to have a 1 % or 2 % probability of failure. The definition is misleading, not only because of the statistical problems of defining these rare conditions, but also because it does not mean that supplies will be maintained in full for the other 99 or 98 years, nor that the supply will ever be allowed to fail completely. As a dry period develops nobody can, at present, forecast when it is going to end and the prudent water supply authority must take precautionary measures to restrict supplies or augment resources in order to conserve its diminishing stocks in storage, even though with hindsight these precautions may be shown to have been unnecessary. This has led the Central Water Planning Unit to consider the concept of expressing reliability in terms of the frequency, duration and severity of restrictions likely to be imposed in practice during any abnormally dry period. The concept poses some difficult methodological problems, but is attractive because it presents the consumer, whether domestic or industrial, with a framework against which he is better able to judge whether the benefit of less severe or less frequent restrictions is worth the cost of the additional works necessary to achieve them. The concept could also provide the water supplier with a means of assessing more explicitly when it is necessary to begin the series of graduated precautionary measures, aimed at keeping consumption and diminishing resources in balance, as a drought period develops.

The concept should, theoretically at least, provide a means of relating the degree of security obtained to the economic consequences of achieving it. Until this ideal is attained, there seems to be no good reason for advocating a radical change from the standards that we have adopted in the past which, although imperfectly defined, have stood the test of time reasonably well.

Much was heard during the drought in 1976 of the benefits that accrued from the ability of the water authorities to provide new links between sources of supply of previously independent water undertakings. The benefits are real and are derived from a number of factors:

1. They can provide a permanent addition to the total yield of the system by physically linking and combining the resources in under-reservoired and over-reservoired catchments.

2. They facilitate the transfer of water from new and hence not fully used resources to augment overloaded resources.

3. They provide for the transfer of supplies between systems in the event of breakdown of either.

Many of these links were being investigated by the water authorities before the drought, and conditions in 1975–76 probably expedited their implementation. All however, depend both now and in the future upon the balance of costs between long and expensive pipelines and the costs of local resource developments.

The same arguments apply to inter-authority transfers that will be developed in the future if they present the economically optimal solution as a permanent addition to resources, or possibly the optimum from a combination of economic and environmental considerations. The fact that they may be able to help to meet drought situations such as those in 1975–76 is a bonus and not the main justification for their implementation.

The case for a national water network must be considered in the same light. The national water grid, referred to frequently during the drought, was conceived not as a system of pipelines covering the whole country in a way analogous to the electricity grid, for this would be prohibitively expensive, but as a limited number of pipeline connections between rivers, existing sources and major aqueducts. In this way resources could be redeployed sequentially across regional boundaries from areas of surplus to areas in need. The elements of such a network already exist in rivers such as the Severn, Thames, Great Ouse and in the major aqueducts linking cities such as Liverpool and Birmingham to reservoirs in Wales, and linking Manchester to the Lake District. It was envisaged that this network could be extended where it was economic to do so, and this is most likely to result from the adoption of inter-authority schemes that can be justified in terms of permanent additions to resources.

In terms of drought insurance, the links will only be of value provided that:

(1) a surplus of resources is available for transfer either because one authority has resources under-utilized, or because of the varying severity of drought conditions over the country;

(2) probably more importantly, that the authority with the apparent surplus has sufficient confidence in its ability to forecast the end of the drought to release supplies that may in the event be needed by their own consumers.

There is no doubt that previous droughts have not affected all areas of the country to the same extent. Figure 6 illustrates that, over the period of record, low flows in the Severn have been generally out of phase with low flows in the Thames. It is a far cry, however, from observing this geographical variability to forecasting its future reoccurrence with sufficient confidence to justify expenditure on elements of a network whose main purpose would be to take advantage of the geographical variability in the incidence of rainfall.

WATER QUALITY

The drought also gave rise to a number of water quality problems. The overriding theme is, however, that these problems were probably not as serious as might have been expected. In rivers, the smaller volume of freshwater flow available to dilute effluents was balanced by smaller sewage flows, due to decreased consumption of water. In addition, sewage treatment works operated better under the smaller flows and in the higher ambient temperatures, which also improved the self-purification capacity of the rivers. Similarly, problems with water treatment were offset to some degree by the spare capacity available at treatment works because of the reductions in consumption.

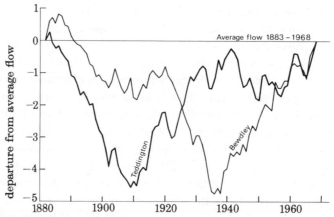

FIGURE 6. Cumulative departure from the long-term average of river flows of the river Thames at Teddington and the river Severn at Bewdley (one unit equals the average annual flow). A fall in value in 1 year compared with the previous year indicates a lower than average flow, as shown by the point for the dry year of 1901 on the plot of the Thames flows; a rise in value indicates a higher than average flow for that particular year.

At the risk of over-simplification, the water quality problems can be separated into two categories: (1) those of an operational nature, and (2) those of funda-mental importance for water resource planning.

(1) The operational problems include:

(a) increased algal growth in eutrophic reservoirs as a result of increased temperature and sunlight;

(b) stratification and poor water quality in the lower levels of reservoirs;

(c) identification of emergency sources, their quality and the provision of emergency treatment plant;

(d) the provision of emergency water supplies where the normal supply failed or its quality made it unsuitable for certain uses;

(e) maintaining the quality of water in the distribution system under reduced pressures and diminished or even discontinued flows.

These and similar problems have been considered by the water authorities who will doubtless deal with them either by strengthening weaknesses in the system or in their contingency planning for future occasions. But few, if any, were of a kind that would suggest the need for a radical change in approach to water resources planning.

(2) Of fundamental importance were:

(*f*) evidence from some rivers that reduced dilution of effluents led to higher levels of persistent organic or inorganic constituents in river-derived supplies;

(*g*) greater concentrations of nitrate in run-off from agricultural land after the heavy rains at the end of the drought;

(*h*) lack of knowledge of the effects of reduction in residual flows on fisheries and ecology generally. On the one hand setting the residual flows too high may lead to a wasteful use of resources and if set too low may lead to long-term ecological damage. Similarly, if residual flows are too frequently raided in periods drier than that for which the water resource system is designed then ecological damage is likely to result.

These problems, which were highlighted by the drought, are symptomatic of longer-term trends or issues on which our basic knowledge is at present inadequate. They indicate areas in which increased effort will be required both in safeguarding our existing supplies and in planning their extension in the future.

FUTURE PLANNING

Consideration of future planning starts from the premise that, on present forecasts, a growth of demand of something less than 2 % p.a. seems firmly established, due largely to a reduction in population forecasts (Central Water Planning Unit 1977*b*).

The water industry is putting a great deal of effort into investigations of water use, water saving appliances, reduction of waste and leakage. Following its experiences of the drought, industry will also be looking at its past practices and may translate some of the savings achieved during the drought into permanent economies. All these efforts should lead to a twofold result, in the first instance that forecasts of demand should be more firmly based on a foundation of better knowledge, but secondly that more efficient water use and reduction of waste will mean that there will be less potential for saving in future drought situations. Arguably, this could lead in the long term to a need for higher standards of reliability. The implications of a change in reliability are that doubling our present reliability standards of about 2 % would mean a proportionate increase in storage requirements of about 20 %. To give some reality to these figures, the present total surface storage in England and Wales is about 2500×10^6 m³. Approximately 500×10^6 m³ of additional storage would be required to double the reliability of our present supply system, or four new reservoirs the size of Empingham. But, as suggested earlier, any dramatic change in standards is not justifiable on present evidence and any change to higher (or lower) standards is more likely to be a gradual transition over a long period. Except in limited areas all essential demands were met even during the drought.

A 2 % growth implies that by 2001 we shall be using only 11 % of our total resources and, if present standards of reliability are maintained, we shall need to develop something like another 900×10^6 m³ of storage to cater for our increased demands. The criteria for development will continue to be the selection of the most economic resource which provides water of the right quality, having full regard to environmental and amenity consequences of the development.

A small growth rate and continuing economic restraint will tend to favour the development of small schemes in which less capital is tied up in under-utilized capacity, except in the rare case, such as the Craig Goch reservoir, where a major inter-authority scheme appears to have overwhelming advantages. In this social and economic climate, water authorities may be expected to continue to explore means of making better use of their present resources by integrating their systems to provide additional yield from existing storage. While much can be done by linking under- and over-reservoired surface catchments, the greatest potential probably lies in linking surface and groundwater resources and the drought enabled several instances of combined use of resources to be utilized.

Traditionally, groundwater has been developed to provide continuous daily supplies to meet local demands. Yield is limited to the long-term annual average rate of recharge and water is drawn from storage within the aquifer only when the rate of abstraction exceeds the rate of recharge. Only in recent years has the concept of using groundwater in combination with surface run-off gained general acceptance, and by using new techniques greater yields can be sustained and greater use made of the storage available in the aquifer (Richards & Downing 1977). The Thames and Anglian Water Authorities' schemes for development of aquifer storage are typical examples of the use of groundwater storage to regulate river flows. Elsewhere, and in other circumstances, it may be more convenient to provide supplies alternately from the river or groundwater source. The net result in terms of increased yield will be much the same, but alternating use, while avoiding the losses usually associated with regulation, may introduce additional problems of duplicate treatment and the effects of varying qualities on consumers and on the distribution system.

A further stage of development is the introduction of artificial recharge. The constraint on development then becomes the storage capacity available rather than the natural annual recharge, but for most of our major aquifers enormous volumes of storage are available which are at present little used. For example, it is estimated that the storage available in the top 50 m of the Bunter Sandstone of Nottinghamshire exceeds 600×10^6 m³, equivalent to five times as much storage as the total surface storage in Britain used for public water supply.

The choice of scale of development then becomes largely economic, balancing the costs of abstraction and recharge works against the alternative surface storage developments. The final stage is deliberate temporary over-exploitation, either as a means of deferring other expensive resource developments, or as a means of providing emergency supplies during conditions such as the 1976 drought. If it constitutes an economic solution, there is no reason why groundwater should not be exploited in this way, provided that the limitations are fully appreciated from the outset. Little of this storage was called upon during the drought of 1976.

By and large, our groundwater resources are at present of good quality but recent trends, both in this country and overseas, give cause for concern and underline the necessity for the most careful control over any discharges that may, in the long term, impair this quality. Two factors must not be forgotten:

(1) that the effects of pollution may take years to become apparent because of the long delay between recharge from the surface, transmission through the unsaturated zone and ultimate abstraction;

(2) that once contaminated, it may take years before a groundwater source can be rehabilitated for reuse as a source for potable supplies.

Pollution of our surface water resources is more easily discernible, but given the hard facts of geography, our industrial society and the costs of effluent treatment, no less difficult to control. Over the years we have come to rely more and more on the provision of water supplies from the lower reaches of rivers which contain sewage or industrial effluents. The reasons have been largely geographical or economic; in the southeast because of the lack of suitable impounding reservoir sites, elsewhere because of the economic benefits that arise from using upland reservoirs to regulate the flow of whole river systems to a downstream abstraction point close to the centre of demand. At present something like one-third of all our present water supplies are derived from such rivers. During the drought river supplies did not worsen materially, perhaps largely because of smaller discharges into them of effluents and of improved quality of those effluents resulting from higher operating temperatures.

In recent years there has been increasing concern relating to the possibility of long-term effects on health from such river-derived supplies. Although no damage to health has been positively linked with the use of river-derived supplies, there is a good deal of uncertainty concerning the nature of the contaminants which may be present. In particular, the range of organic compounds which may occur in effluents has increased enormously in recent years and they now number several thousands. Although the concentrations of these compounds are usually small, not enough is known of their possible effects on human health. Much research work is in hand in the U.K. and abroad, particularly in the United States, and the problem is being tackled energetically by the water authorities, particularly in the Thames and Anglian areas where the problems are greatest. This and other water quality problems, such as nitrate and lead contents, underline the predominance of water quality rather than quantity problems in future water resource planning.

Summary

Future trends in water resource planning may be summarized as follows:

(a) Increasing attention to studies of water use and control of waste with a view to more efficient water use and better forecasts of demand. Control of demand by more effective water-using appliances and the possibility of control by pricing.

(b) More detailed hydrological assessments and the design of operating rules with particular attention to the benefits that may be derived from the combined use of different sources.

(c) Increasing attention to environmental, amenity and recreational aspects of water resource developments.

(d) More detailed studies of appropriate reliability standards and their implications for the consumer.

(e) Increasing attention to quality problems, in particular those associated with reuse of river water containing sewage and industrial effluents.

Of these, combined use, reliability and the quality problems of river-derived supplies were highlighted rather than identified by the 1975–76 drought.

REFERENCES (Gibb & Richards)

Central Water Planning Unit 1977a *The 1975–76 drought: a hydrological review*. Technical Note 17.
Central Water Planning Unit 1977b *Public water supply in 1975 and trends in consumption*. Technical Note 19.
Drought Act 1976 (14 pages.) London: H.M.S.O.
Mason, B. J. 1976 Towards the understanding and prediction of climatic variations. *Q. Jl R. met. Soc.* **102**, 473–498.
National Water Council 1977 *The 1975–76 drought*. London: N.W.C.
Richards, H. J. & Downing, R. A. 1977 Aquifer management in England and Wales. *Memoires of Birmingham Congress of Int. Assoc. Hydrogeologists*, vol. 13, pp. G30–G53.
Rowntree, N. A. F. 1961 Rainfall and runoff at reservoired catchments in 1959. *J. Inst. Wat. Engrs* **15**, 151–2.
Tabony, R. C. 1977 *The variability of long-duration rainfall over Great Britain*. Meteorological Office Scientific Paper No. 37. H.M.S.O. 40 pages.
Water Resources Board 1974 *Tenth annual report*. London: H.M.S.O.
Water Resources Board 1973 *Water resources in England and Wales*. London: H.M.S.O.
Wright, C. E. 1976 Once in 1,000 years? *Water* **11**, 2–6.

Proc. R. Soc. Lond. A, **363**, 131–133 (1978)

Printed in Great Britain

Concluding remarks

By Sir Charles Pereira, F.R.S.

Formerly Ministry of Agriculture, Fisheries and Food, London, U.K.

This meeting was called one full year after the official ending of the drought, in order to give time for full analysis and study of the data. We had, entirely by chance, picked the date which is statistically the wettest day of the wettest week in the year.

In a one-day discussion it was not possible to cover all subjects and I was glad to receive from the Nature Conservancy Council an excellent report by Katherine Hearn and Michael Gilbert on the effects of the drought on Britain's natural ecology. Observations on 350 National Nature Reserves and Sites of Special Scientific Interest had shown a general picture of rapid recovery, except where fire had severely damaged some 50 of these areas. Their main fear was of the extra water-development activities involving abstractions and riverbank training which might be stimulated by the drought.

The one-year wait was richly rewarded by an excellent set of papers, with a valuable and authentic tabulation of reference data in the bulletin of abstracts.

From the masterly presentation of the meteorological analysis by Mr Ratcliffe and his colleagues of the Meteorological Office there seems to be a cautious note of optimism that we are moving a step or two closer to an understanding of the mechanisms of climate variability. First, all of the Meteorological Office indicators suggested that the drought should end early in 1976, but the drought had created the conditions for a 'feedback' effect by which its existence was prolonged. Mr Ratcliffe has explained this as an increase in the albedo of the landscape. This situation is exaggerated in the tropics, especially where drought is accentuated by land misuse of overgrazing in areas of several hundred square kilometres, as in the Sahel. Mr Ratcliffe's illustrations of modelling studies demonstrate that the persistence both of droughts and of wet weather can be increased by feedback effects. He also confirms the suspicions of the public that the exceptionally heavy autumn rains were due in some way to the drought, by the simple explanation of the uptake of extra water vapour from an unusually warm sea surface around Britain.

The second area in which knowledge has advanced is that of the involvement of the surface temperatures of the Pacific Ocean. This gives us an increased priority for the use of more scientific resources for recording of ocean temperatures. Mr Ratcliffe was emphatic that tests at 5 day, monthly, quarterly or annual intervals had shown neither evidence of climatic trends nor indication of greater variability. The 1975–76 drought lay within the range of events which could be expected to recur.

Mr Clarke and Mr Newson have given a summary of the first six years' results from one of the world's most intensive studies of catchment-area hydrology. The study of the basic processes of reception, distribution, storage and use of water under the two most important land uses, forestry and sheep pasture, is providing information which can indeed be applied scientifically to other catchments. Only by taking into account slope, soil depth, and percentage of forest cover can effective comparisons be made, but much of the controversy about such work consists of crude generalizations. Dr Clarke states that if the whole of a grassed headwater catchment were fully afforested then the increased water use, usually due more to interception losses than to transpiration, would require provision of extra reservoir capacity as an insurance against exceptional drought. In the very dry conditions of 1975 and 1976 interception losses from the trees were lower, but transpiration losses were increased. Afforestation in similar mountain catchments in Wales usually occupied only 20–30 % of the headwaters area.

Mr Carter has described the agricultural effects of the drought. Soil moisture deficits were serious over the catchment areas south of a line from Humber to Mersey. Grain yields were reduced by about one tonne per hectare to about three-quarters of the normal harvest, while main-crop potatoes were reduced from 75 to 50 tonnes per hectare. The effects were thus economically serious, but by no means disastrous. Aphid populations were large and troublesome. Irrigation responses were profitable and the need for more irrigation development, as consistently advised by M.A.F.F., became very apparent. Two signs of the almost tropical temperatures were difficulties in sustaining work in glasshouses, and the appearance of rice-weevils in our grain stores. Farmers kept their livestock fed only with great difficulty and much expensive additional imports of grain. There was a fall in both livestock numbers and milk yield. On the whole, however, the British farming industry showed great enterprise and resilience in meeting these exceptional conditions. The difficulties caused by the heavy autumn rains were, for farmers struggling to lift potatoes and sugar beet from muddy fields, often greater than those of the drought. Drainage was even more important than irrigation on heavy soils.

Mr Carter has commented on the very serious implications for British agriculture if such wet autumns recurred more frequently, since most of our grain crops are sown before winter.

Mr Day, in his joint paper with Dr Rodda, has emphasized the importance of groundwater sources, which were estimated to have produced one-third of the national supply at the height of the drought. By a rapid review of typical hydrographs they show that only the top layer, of about 10 % of the capacity, was exhausted during the drought. This left an immense storage capacity which was untapped. New developments of pumping to storage, and of recharging from surplus streamflow, on both the Thames and the Anglian rivers, are demonstrating the potential value of these underground reservoirs. However, Mr Day warns that after prolonged pumping the draw-down of underground water levels reduces the yield of springs, so that net yield reaches a limiting value.

Professor Hamlin, in his joint paper with Mr Wright, has demonstrated the complexity of the Water Authorities' problems from the behaviour of eight river systems during the drought. He emphasizes that comparisons should be by river flow data rather than by rainfall records. The drought had widely different effects on the various river systems, so that many of the alarming generalizations presented to the public in the news media were misleading.

Mr Davies, dealing with water quality from the users' viewpoint, suggests that the full effects may not be known for another two or three years. He gives rather an alarming account of the accumulation of dust, debris in channels, farm residues on the soil surface and other accumulated pollution which was washed into the reservoirs with the first heavy rains. In spite of these hazards the quality of the public supplies was maintained. The self-purification effects of increased reservoir storage played an important part, and the sheer dilution effects of the very heavy autumn rains cleared up most of the problems. Mr Davies foresees increased problems with pollution by nitrates in the major chalk and gravel aquifers, but he emphasizes that this needs more research. Some Water Authorities were already experimenting with deionization plants for removal of nitrates.

In the final paper Mr Gibb and Mr Richards emphasized that Britain does indeed have enough water resources to meet all foreseeable needs. The reliability of public daily supplies, however, depends directly on how much the people are prepared to pay for storage. The results of past foresight, or of past opposition to developments, whether from financial or ecological considerations, left the authorities in different regions facing the drought either with confidence or with known inadequacy of reserves. Mr Gibb suggests that a better way of presenting the case to the public would be to state the probability of disruption of water supplies at different levels of inconvenience. For the future, the growth of demand is slowing unexpectedly, and a total increase of 12 % by the end of the century is probable. It is well within our capacity to develop from known resources.

In concluding this summary of the outstanding points of the day's discussion, I am confident that the meeting showed how well the unique opportunity was being taken to study the meteorological, hydrological, hydrogeological and agricultural effects of the drought. From the point of view of the public the scientific message was reassuring. The most severe drought for 200 years tested our defences in both water supply and food supply from our countryside. In both cases damage was sustained but the defences held good.